Seoul

This book focuses on understanding how a megacity like Seoul can be read as a formal architectural composition and not an endless urban sprawl.

In a broader sense, the book discusses the dichotomy between city and urbanization: "city" being an architectural problem of bounded forms, while "urbanism" is an infrastructural project of expansion. It is an uncontested reality that urbanization is a continuous global process that has produced nebulous conurbations labeled as megacities. These expand beyond the virtual administrative boundary of any said "city," producing a discrepancy between an area of administrative control and the real physical condition of human settlement. If there were a better formal understanding of megacities through their typological architectural conditions, then there could be a better assessment of the qualitative state of urbanization. Avant-garde groups from the 1950s, 1960s, and 1970s such as Team X, the Situationist, the Structuralist, and the Metabolist worked with ideas of megaforms and megastructures to address this issue. Although most of these proposals remained as paper architecture, this book reevaluates some of these ideas for the 21st-century megacity, using Seoul as a case study due to its clear typological formations produced over its different periods of governance. The aim is to present the concept for an infra-architectural hybrid model of typological islands and subterranean megastructure that organizes Seoul as a flexible multi-linear city.

This book will be of interest to academics and students of architecture, urban geography, and Asian studies.

Rafael Luna is the co-founder of the architecture firm PRAUD, a senior lecturer at the University of Technology Sydney, and the director of the Infra-Architecture Lab. He received a master of architecture from the Massachusetts Institute of Technology (2010) and his Ph.D. in architecture focused on infra-architectural typologies as urban models from L'Accademia di architettura dell'Università della Svizzera italiana, Mendrisio, Switzerland (2022). Luna is the award winner of the Architectural League Prize 2013, and his work has been exhibited at the MoMA, Venice Biennale, and Seoul Biennale. Luna was a co-curator of the Cities Exhibition for the 2019 Seoul Biennale, awarded by the Mayor of Seoul. He has professional experience from the offices of Toyo Ito and Associates, KPF, Ateliers Jean Nouvel, Martha Schwartz Partners, dECOI, Sasaki Associates, and Machado and Silvetti. He served as an assistant professor at Hanyang University from 2018 to 2022, previously teaching at the Rhode Island School of Design. His writings have been published in journals such as G+L, Topos, MONU, SPACE, and IntAR Journal, and he was a guest editor for AD magazine's September 2021 issue *Production Urbanism: The Meta-Industrial City*. He is the co-author of *I Want to Be Metropolitan*, the *North Korean Atlas* (received the DAM award), and *A Language of Contemporary Architecture: An Index of Topology and Typology.*

Built Environment City Studies

The *Built Environment City Studies* series provides researchers and academics with a detailed look at individual cities through a specific lens. These concise books delve into a case study of an international city, focusing on a key built environment topic. Written by scholars from around the world, the collection provides a library of thorough studies into trends, developments and approaches that affect our cities.

Glasgow
High-Rise Homes, Estates and Communities in the Post-War Period
Lynn Abrams, Ade Kearns, Barry Hazley and Valerie Wright

Pemba
Spontaneous Living Spaces
Corinna Del Bianco

Vienna
Still a Just City?
Edited by Yuri Kazepov and Roland Verwiebe

Havana
Mapping Lived Experiences of Urban Agriculture
Susan Fitzgerald

Seoul
Of Islands and Megastructures
Rafael Luna

For more information about this series, please visit: www.routledge.com/Built-Environment-City-Studies/book-series/BECS

Seoul
Of Islands and Megastructures

Rafael Luna

LONDON AND NEW YORK

First published 2024
by Routledge
4 Park Square, Milton Park, Abingdon, Oxon OX14 4RN

and by Routledge
605 Third Avenue, New York, NY 10158

Routledge is an imprint of the Taylor & Francis Group, an informa business

British Library Cataloguing-in-Publication Data
A catalogue record for this book is available from the British Library

ISBN: 978-1-032-68494-9 (hbk)
ISBN: 978-1-032-68495-6 (pbk)
ISBN: 978-1-032-68496-3 (ebk)

DOI: 10.4324/9781032684963

Typeset in Times New Roman
by Apex CoVantage, LLC

This book is an homage for my everlasting fascination to Seoul and South Korea in general. In that sense, I am dedicating this book to my family; to my parents who first introduced me to Korea over two decades ago, shaping what would be my appreciation for Korean culture, and to my wife and kids, whose love and adventurous spirits made Seoul home.

Contents

Figures

Acknowledgments

I would like to thank my partner Dongwoo Yim, who helped me in discussing the problems, issues, and different points of view that this book could take.

To Prof. Dr. Sonja Hildebrand and Prof. Dr. Sascha Roesler, who helped me shape this research with insightful comments and discussions.

A special thanks to my colleagues at Hanyang University. Sung Taeg Nam for constantly checking on my progress. Jae Kyung Kim for presenting me with the opportunity to do research at Hanyang. Keehyun Ahn for allowing me to have freedom in developing the research. To all my students at Hanyang University who helped with the fieldwork, and my TAs, Eun Hyung Cho, and Bumsoo Cho for helping me organize the data and materials. To Annie Pedret who helped me from the start formulating the research question and providing critiques.

1 Introduction

Understanding Seoul in the Context of Urbanization

What sort of significant and critical relationship can architecture aspire to in a world that is no longer constituted by the idea and the motivation of the city, but is instead dominated by urbanization?[1]

The ongoing project of urbanization is continuously presented through satellite imagery such as the NASA vision of the Earth at night that reflects an ever-expanding infrastructural network, illuminating connected conurbations. Pairing with this imagery, the hardly contested data from the United Nations (UN)[2] with regard to urbanization portrays a global population that is overwhelmingly becoming more urban.[3] Within this context, the introductory question (from Pier Vittorio Aureli) points out a distinction to be made between the terms "city" and "urbanization." From the question, it can be deduced that these terms are not to be used interchangeably as they represent a very distinct context for the role of architecture within them. The project of city making can be related to architecture,[4] while urbanization is a project of an ever-expanding human settlement and is manifested through infrastructure as proposed by Catalan planner Ildefons Cerdà in his *General Theory of Urbanization*.[5] When Cerdà proposed the *Eixample* for Barcelona in the second half of the 19th century, he aimed at distributing the density from the medieval city center into the surrounding landscape by means of an engineered infrastructural grid that would allow for a continuous expansion. This was done to accommodate the increasing population that was moving from rural agricultural areas into city centers as industrialization formed a new economy with new labor markets in the 19th century. Urbanization started shaping society through political, economical, social, and technological dimensions by means of infrastructural networks that facilitated new particular lifestyles. Urban expansion continued in the 20th century, and by the 21st century the UN identified cities with over ten million inhabitants as megacities, presented through their World Urbanization Prospects report every year since 2008.[6] Yet, the new label for megacities is challenged by the NASA image of "Earth at Night" that shows how difficult it is to formally identify said megacities since

DOI: 10.4324/9781032684963-1

urban sprawl has expanded beyond administrative boundaries. If there were a better formal understanding of megacities as bounded elements rather than endless sprawling urbanization, then it could facilitate managing resources and producing equitable sustainable developments. Avant-garde architecture groups like Team X, the Situationist, the Structuralist, and the Metabolist foresaw a problem with the modern models of urbanization and conceptualized how architecture could take a role in organizing large formations. Although most of these proposals remain as paper architecture, perhaps their abstract concepts could present a contemporary architectural solution for the question: Can architecture have a role in defining a clear idea of form at an extra-large urban scale that properly identifies city form in a megacity as opposed to sprawling urbanization?

Urbanization trends by the UN have tracked Asia and the Pacific as areas of fast and vast urbanization.[7] Twenty-nine cities out of forty-seven megacities identified by the UN in 2021 are located in Asia.[8] Among these megacities, Seoul has had a unique historical development, which consisted of radical periods of governance, with distinct agendas that influenced how the built space was formed accounting for rapid population growth for each period. This created a layering process of architectural typological formations in Seoul that reflected each epoch of governance and the demographic needs of the time from its inception, more than 600 years ago, to the present. By focusing on Seoul's urban morphology through these architectural typologies, Seoul can be understood as an organized architectural formation rather than formless urban sprawl.

A Brief Introduction to Seoul

While Seoul has a massive metropolitan area, this book focuses on the area within the administrative boundary of the city of Seoul and its 25 *Gu* (districts). Seoul presents the perfect condition for exploring "typological urbanism"[9] due to its drastic changes in governance within its 625 years of existence that produced variants in typologies and urban fabrics that were highly documented through mapping and still exist today as different layers in the city allowing for firsthand observations.

The progression that occurs from the foundation of Seoul in 1394 to its present day megapolitan condition can be separated into five phases: Hanyang as the capital of the Joseon Dynasty (1394–1897), Hanseong as the capital of the Daehan Empire (1897–1910), Gyeongseong as the colonial capital (1910–1945), Seoul as the industrial capital (1953–1988), Seoul as the global capital (1988–2002), and Seoul as the cultural capital (2002–present). Each transitional phase of Seoul was directly linked to a specific political and economic agenda and shifts in population density that produced different urban fabrics through architectural typologies.

Shortly after the foundation of the Joseon Dynasty in 1392, a new capital was built in 1394 as the new center of the kingdom. This initial city had an infrastructural organization that followed geomancy principles, and its architecture served the ritualistic operations of the king.[10] Two observable typologies came from this period – the royal grounds produced political forms, and the generic urban fabric mostly made up of single-family *hanoks* that infilled the compacted area inside the city walls with about 17,000 homes for about 100,000 people.[11]

In 1867, King Gojong declared the formation of the Daehan Empire proclaiming the Gwangmu Reforms in order to open the hermit state to the modernities of the West.[12] As foreign economic treaties were signed, a new architectural typology was introduced – the iconic form (landmark buildings). In Seoul, these were Western style legation buildings, separated from the generic urban fabric as stand-alone autonomous buildings that served to foment the foreign alliances.[13] This typology produced a more sparse urbanity in a city that now reached a population of about 200,000 people.[14]

The expansion of the city continued during the Japanese forceful occupation. This period starting in 1910 looked to continue the modernization reforms using the Meiji Restorations done in Tokyo and Osaka as a model for the colonial capital and used as a tool for an assimilation process toward the Japanese Empire.[15] The reforms symbolized control over the colony and were constructed through a wave of slum clearing projects in order to modernize the city with new infrastructures. The neoclassical Government General Building completed in 1926, for example, was a clear imposition to the old Joseon structure by disrupting the main axis of the city and blocking Gyeongbokgung palace. The Old City Hall building built in 1925 in an Imperial Crown Style is another example that exists until today. Its autonomy in the fabric led to the urban void, which was transformed into Seoul City Hall Plaza in 2002.

The independence of Korea after the fall of the Japanese Empire was quickly followed by the Korean War from 1950 to 1953, which left Seoul in an impoverished and devastated state. After the armistice of 1953, the immigration from rural to urban rapidly surged, creating unplanned squatter settlements.[16] Park Chung Hee assumed power in 1963 and shifted the country's economic focus to an export-oriented industrialization producing rapid economic growth.[17] With the 1960s policies of heavy industrialization, this immigration flourished at a rate of 300,000 people per year by the 1970s.[18] Annexation projects, slum clearing projects, and large infrastructure projects were proposed by the government as the urban growth continued in the fringe areas. This pressure for housing led to land speculation and urban growth south of the Han River with gridded patterns that formed superblocks and large apartment complexes that followed a Western development style in order to achieve housing density at great speed.[19] The need for mass housing quickly became a primary agenda that resulted in mid and high-rise single-use slab housing block typology and the *Sangga* mixed-use developments characterized by their megaform.

The need for housing construction sponsored by the government drove the scale of projects focused on quantity. Single developments were in charge of 1,000–2,000 units distributed in multiple slab buildings in the same parcel of land.[20] As a new development strategy using land owned by the government, Kim Swoo Geun is commissioned to design Seun Sangga. Influenced by the teachings of Kenzo Tange, Kim Swoo Geun plans for a megastructure to span over four city blocks, exploring the three dimensionality of the city on a site that was left as a fire barrier from the Japanese occupation. The megastructure consisted of an elevated pedestrian deck that would connect the four blocks with 2,000 retail and office spaces, a hotel with 177 rooms, and 851 apartment units.[21] More megastructures followed such as Nagwon Arcade and Yujin Sangga combining infrastructure and architecture as a singular project. Along the Cheonggyecheon, Pyeonghwa market and Shin Pyeonghwa Fashion Town were developed as 200 m long buildings running parallel to the stream forming a military barrier and at the same time becoming hubs of fashion production and retail centers.

The 1988 Olympics became a driving force for showcasing the city as a modern metropolis. During this period two more block typologies were developed: the tower block with the 63 building as the prime example and the deep block with the emergence of megamalls by three leading retail developers – Shinsegae, Hyundai, and Lotte. Corporate towers took over the Central Business District as a redevelopment strategy for urban slum clearing. Large corporations were given rights to parcels in the center of the city with the condition that they develop the infrastructure of the block for their corporate headquarters as towers. COEX was developed as a mall and convention center, taking over a megablock in Gangnam to display a globalized Seoul that could offer international brands and be a host for international commerce. The Jamsil Sports Complex was completed as the grounds for the Olympics featuring state-of-the-art monumental stadiums. Large infrastructural projects such as the subway system (1974) and the Olympic Expressway (1986) were developed to cope with the increasing vehicular congestion. Gangnam expands its developments following an 800 m × 800 m megablocks system based on the Basic Seoul Urban Plan.[22] The main streets of the megablocks were bundled with the subway system and infrastructural conduits to create main avenues.

By the turn of the century, the rapid urban development that had pushed the population to ten million in a city of 605 km^2 had also pushed production and industry outside of the city. Housing blocks had become monocultured islands in the large megalopolis. This phenomenon was quickly recognized, and toward the end of the century a new sentiment was brewing to transform the city from an industrial city of growth to a post-industrial "cultural capital." In her book *Globalizing Seoul*,[23] Jieheerah Yun makes an argument for Seoul being shaped by a globalization effort, "Segyehwa," that developed Seoul into a global hub, and as a consequence, globalization shaped its urban spatial context led by policies of rapid industrialization. Since the 2000s Seoul has switched from this idea of being a global city to being a "cultural" city – from a heavy industrial city to a cosmopolitan one. Yun makes the claim that the idea of the cultural city became the discourse in the early 2000s when the Seoul Development Institute published a study in 2002 regarding the urban state of Seoul, in which they suggested that Seoul needed to cultivate cultural spaces.[24] The study described Seoul's urban spaces as not being conducive to the cultivation of cultures. There should be a focus on cultural industries as opposed to manufacturing industries and promote a higher quality of life. This is not a new concept, as it had already been defined in 1985 by the European Capital of Culture Programme started by Melina Mercouri and Jack Lang, the ministers of culture from Greece and France, respectively. As explained by the European Commission report for European Capitals of Culture (ECOC) bids from 2020 to 2033,

> Since the 1980s there has been steadily growth in the awareness of the role of culture in the life of cities: its contribution to citizens' well-being and to the prosperity of a city, as well as its potential to reinforce a city's positioning on the international map. Many of the cities which have held the ECOC title have not only had a successful year but have benefitted from a lasting legacy.[25]

This called for a cultivation of environments that were conducive to cultural activities. According to this concept, Seoul needed to change from an industrial city focused on speed and efficiency to a cultural city that showed appreciation for its traditional cultures.

This has had a profound effect in the way the city started valuing its infrastructure, building stock, and industrial relationship inside the city, which led to new housing models, a move toward preserving cultural enclaves with cultural blocks, and the optimization of its infrastructural spaces. In an almost live version of Koolhaas's "The City of the Captive Globe,"[26] the podium typology emerged in the 1990s and early 2000s as a new model for mixed use. Each podium base represents an entire block that houses commercial retail and offices, while on top of the podium slab housing towers stand as independent pieces of architecture. In parallel, the underground systems built in the 1970s consisting of subway tunnels and underground pedestrian crosswalks evolved as programmable commercial areas such as Myeongdong Underground Shopping District or Yeongdeungpo Underground Shopping District. More than just transportation infrastructure, this underground network became a second layer for the city as an underground architecture (infra-architecture in its literal meaning).

The transformation of infrastructures as new public spaces became more noticeable from Lee Myung-bak's term as mayor from 2002 to 2006, when he implemented urban infrastructure transformation projects in order to soften the cityscape. His most notable projects were adapting the Cheonggyecheon stream into a public landscaped recreational space through the city center.[27] He also transformed a vehicular roundabout in front of the City Hall into a grassy field that would serve as a plaza for public events and gatherings. Seoul Forest Park was also developed during his administration, creating a natural reserve public park that would serve as a new lung for the city. These changes have continued post Mayor Lee's administration through a series of open international competitions that focus on these cultural urban spaces. One of the most controversial being the development of the Dongdaemun Design Plaza by Zaha Hadid. In order to transform Dongdaemun as a new design node and attractor, the city decided to demolish two outdated stadiums, displace street vendors, and construct a new cultural center. Despite the criticism for its lack of functionality, "the role of the building as a landmark and a tool for economic revitalization played a greater part than that of service provision."[28] Following the completion of the Dongdaemun Design Plaza a new series of competitions emerged. Seosomun Memorial Museum and Park competition in 2014 looked at redeveloping an urban park as a historic, cultural, and religious space. Sejong-daero Historic Cultural Space Design Competition in 2015 called for the design of a new public cultural space across City Hall connecting to the underground. One of the most significant competitions was the adaptive reuse of the Seun Sangga megastructure. From the brief,

> The objective of the "Re-Structuring Seun Sangga Citywalk" competition in Seoul is to renovate the deck and nearby public space of Seun Sangga Complex to improve the pedestrian environment and connect with surrounding areas of various nature and thereby re-establish a pedestrian axis from north to south through Bugaksan Mountain, Jongmyo~Seun Sangga Complex, and Namsan Mountain. Not only is Seun Sangga Complex Seoul's "urban-architectural heritage," it is a compound of history, culture and industry that connects the surrounding area and various activities.

The following year in 2016 the Nodeul Dream Island Competition sought to transform an island on the Han River as a music cultural center. Mayor Park Won-Soon commissioned MVRDV to transform and reuse an existing vehicular overpass into a pedestrian cultural bridge that connects Seoul Station to Namdaemun Market, which opened in 2017.[29] These projects shed a brighter light on the transformation of infrastructure as architectural hybrids that operate as part of the commons of the city. This sentiment is evident with the competition to design Gwanghwamun Plaza (one of the most iconic cultural spaces of the city) as an underground connection to the subway and its surrounding buildings and the competition for the Intermodal Transit Center in Gangnam won by Dominique Perrault.[30]

Industry has also been able to come back into the city under the umbrella of culture. Under the governance of Mayor Park Won-Soon, "Sharing City Seoul"[31] project was initiated to give rise to the sharing economy and optimize the use of the city and address the fourth industrial revolution of the Internet of Things.

The State of Urbanization

This brief recap of the history of Seoul is meant to illustrate the strong correlation that can occur between the growth of a city and specific architectural typological formations, which could show an architectural reading of the city of Seoul. The value in this analysis is to form a new strategy for how architecture can organize large urban forms, especially with the current state of what seems a planetary urbanization.

In a modern context, the transition from city form to urbanization largely influenced architectural research during the 20th century. Some of the investigations that emerged from the avant-garde groups from the 1950s, 1960s, and 1970s dealt with megaforms, megastructures, and collective forms as a way for architecture to deal with the new urban paradigm where infrastructure had become the predominant tool. In the earlier half of the 20th century though, the transition in focus from architecture to infrastructure is palpable, for example, when comparing Ludwig Hilberseimer's 1924 Vertical City theoretical proposal for Berlin to his proposed plan for Chicago from 1944.

While the project for Berlin, Vertical City, proposed architecture as the means to produce urban blocks through a repeatable vertical typology, his proposal for Chicago focused on infrastructural organizations where the sense of city form is lost and only infrastructure remains in the imagery. His proposals indicated a clear deviation from architecture as a tool for city making to an infrastructural urban growth strategy.

Seeing this transition, the project of urbanization was radically conceptualized by Constantinos Doxiadis as a global phenomenon. Based on his research on Ekistics, in 1961, Constantinos Doxiadis coined the term "Ecumenopolis" to describe a unified continuous settlement across the globe, which he later published in 1974 as *Ecumenopolis: The Inevitable City of the Future*.[32] In his book, Doxiadis begins to describe an era of megapolitan expansion that can be already observed not only through the aforementioned NASA satellite imagery of the world at night but also through political and economic policies that agglomerate large economic zones linking multiple cities such as BeNeLux or the BosWash corridor. Cities that were once quite formal like Sao Paulo, Tokyo, and Mexico City have developed into amorphous conurbations agglomerated as metropolitan regions. In China for example, the conurbation presents a systematic approach of organization at different scales between large urban nodes and rural towns. The rural in this context is not present in the traditional sense. It is integrated into the larger urban nodes as part of an agrarian urban pixelation where rural towns repeat every kilometer.

Environmental historian William Cronnon wrote in 1996,

> For many Americans wilderness stands as the last remaining place where civilization, that all too human disease, has not fully infected the earth. It is an island in the polluted sea of urban-industrial modernity, the one place we can turn for escape from our own too-muchness.[33]

Although written from an American perspective, the continuous urbanization led by an expansive infrastructural network that crosses geopolitical boundaries formed the bases for studies that have been labeled as planetary urbanization, recognizing this as a global phenomenon.[34] Benjamin Bratton makes the case for a planetary computational framework that has already become an accidental megastructure at a global scale.[35] In this virtual context, the idea of "the city" has increasingly become even more dubious and nebulous.

Urbanism and an Architectural Reaction

For the 21st century, the focus on infrastructure rather than architecture as a macro-organizer of cities begs to ask the question again, "what is the role of architecture under these conditions?" Addressing this question, Xaveer de Geyter Architects would publish their research, *After Sprawl: Research on the Contemporary City*[36] in 2002, illustrating the current urbanization condition in Europe as one that resembles the envisioned Ecumenopolis. Architecture is nonexistent, only to be presented as an accumulation of scaleless fields of urban patches, indistinguishable from one another and noncontextual. Acting on this, a series of proposals are made where architecture intervenes in the urban sea through a manipulation of voids that achieve a sense of organization, directionality, and form – voids acting as urban islands. Architecture, in this sense, is approached through distanciation or separation from its context.

Much of the concept of the architectural island can be attributed to the works of O. M. Ungers and Koolhaas from the 1970s that led to the development of *Berlin: A Green Archipelago*[37] in 1977. The project looked at re-establishing a sense of order in post-war Berlin by evaluating nodes that were still working well in the city. These nodes could be concentrated through a typological grouping in order to create the micro-city (the city within a city) effect. While establishing the concept of the island as an architectural typology reflected a viable strategy for dealing with the issue of a continuous urbanization for de Geyter and Aureli, Ungers would use it as a "shrinking city" strategy. This would mean that the island represents an autonomous entity rather than an urbanization model. It would not matter if the island sits in the middle of an urban sea or a desert. The concept was revisited by Pier

Vittorio Aureli in 2011 through *The Possibility of an Absolute Architecture*. The book reflects on the works of Mies van der Rohe, Hilberseimer, Palladio, Piranesi, Boullée, Koolhaas, and Ungers as architects that implemented architectural strategies of separation to achieve an "absolute" separate condition. For instance, the use of the podium by Mies van der Rohe would separate his buildings from the rest of urbanity by producing a new ground for which to place his buildings. The podium would create a demarcation, a boundary between architecture and urbanization offering a way for architecture to stand out within the urban sphere.

While the architectural island offered a strategy for urban architecture, a parallel concept was growing out of the recognition that infrastructure was instrumental for the project of urbanization. This is attributed to the 20th century planning manifestos, where the role of city making as a physical entity transitioned to other fields such as urban planning and engineering. Under these professions, the idea of city making became more preoccupied with efficiency models of operations rather than quality of urban space. Engaging infrastructure as a potential architectural toolbox, Stan Allen published *Points + Lines: Diagrams and Projects for the City*[38] in 1999, presenting a model for infrastructural urbanism. In order to engage the city through the technical dimension of infrastructure, infrastructural urbanism proposes projects that give a new sense of urban order through the use of expansive green networks that could operate as collective spaces, environmental infrastructure, and urban form. The notion of using infrastructure as green networks deviated more into Landscape Urbanism, led by Charles Waldheim and James Corner,[39] where landscape is utilized for the organization of urban growth. While landscape in Landscape Urbanism is engineered to sustain urban ecologies, support water management, and provide urban form, it is still within the realm of landscape architecture and not a cross-categorical hybrid condition between architecture and civil infrastructure. Hence, the proposal of using infrastructure as an architectural hybrid, as denoted by Stan Allen, still remains to be explored as an architectural artifact in order for architects to have an additional tool to engage urbanism from within the field of architecture. This makes it imperative to review models of urbanization from an architectural typology lens in relation to infrastructure and city form. The 20th century has been attributed as the epoch that delinked architecture from the project of city making, yet it is also a century marked with transitional theoretical debates between city function and counter projects that can be attributed to birthing *infrastructural architectural hybrid* through conceptual projects such as Hilberseimer's theoretical Vertical City project for Berlin published in 1927,[40] Peter and Allison Smithsons' conceptual competition entry for the Golden Lane project in 1952, Constant's hypothetical New Babylon from the 1960s, Kenzo Tange's visionary unbuilt Metabolist projects, Josic Candilis and Woods proposals on Structuralism, or Paul Rudolph's proposal for LOWMEX from 1967. These theoretical projects tried to understand a systematic infrastructural approach for architecture to engage urbanism and the city. It is worth revisiting these theoretical projects from the mid-20th century as infra-architectural hybrids in the context of Seoul due to its higher urban population, higher building densities, and updated construction technologies. Infra-architectural hybrids are projects that tried to understand the city not as a separation of functions in a two-dimensional plane but as an intertwined network of bundled infrastructures in a three-dimensional volume that offered a higher efficiency in urbanity and city form.

By Rossi's terms in the *Architecture of the City*, the city could be understood as "a 'gigantic man-made' structure that merges engineering and architecture."[41] While the architectural islands and the megastructure proposals may have not worked independently to produce urbanization models due to their autonomy, scale, and perhaps their Western context in the 1960s, in the 21st century megalopolis of East Asia, these models (islands and infra-architecture) may already be operational and working in symbiosis with these highly dense, technologically advanced environments. For example, publication such as *Cities Without Ground: A Hong Kong Guidebook*[42] reviews the three dimensionality and interconnectivity that occurs in Hong Kong by means of pedestrian networks that form megastructures linking buildings throughout several blocks. Atelier Bow Wow's *Made in Tokyo*[43] discusses the effects of Tokyo's density on producing unique typologies that optimize the use of real estate through hybrid conditions. Highly developed Asian cities have also invested largely on mass-transit systems that allow efficient connectivity through these expansive urban zones. Seoul presents these conditions, and hence, studying the possibility of these theories not only still being in existence but also remaining pertinent to understanding the megapolitan condition seems to represent a valuable study for the planetary state of urbanization.

Notes

1 Aureli, Pier Vittorio. *The Possibility of an Absolute Architecture*. Cambridge, MA: MIT Press, 2011, p. 2.
2 "68% of the World Population Projected to Live in Urban Areas by 2050, Says UN | UN Desa Department of Economic and Social Affairs." *United Nations*, United Nations, 16 May 2018, www.un.org/development/desa/en/news/population/2018-revision-of-world-urbanization-prospects.html.
3 Angel, Shlomo, et al. "[Re]Form: New Investigations in Urban Form, Panel 2." *YouTube*, Harvard GSD, 26 Sept. 2018, https://youtu.be/a2Rai AORKks.
4 Rossi, Aldo. *The Architecture of the City*. Cambridge, MA: MIT Press, 2007.
5 Cerdá Ildefonso. *Teoría General De La urbanización y aplicación De Sus Principios y Doctrinas a La Reforma y Ensanche De Barcelona*, vol. 1. Madrid: Imprenta Española, 1867.
6 "World Urbanization Prospects 2018 – More Megacities in the Future | Multimedia Library – United Nations Department of Economic and Social Affairs." *United Nations*, United Nations, 16 May 2018, www.un.org/

development/desa/publications/graphic/world-urbanization-prospects-2018-more-megacities-in-the-future.

7 ESCAP. "Urbanization Trends in Asia and the Pacific." *United Nations*, Nov. 2013, www.unescap.org/sites/default/files/SPPS-Factsheet-urbanization-v5.pdf.

8 "Megacities Worldwide | UNESCO." *Second International Conference on Water, Megacities and Global Change*, UNESCO, 2021, https://en.unesco.org/events/eaumega2021/megacities.

9 Lee, Christopher C. M., and Sam Jacoby. "Typological Urbanism and the Idea of the City." *Architectural Design*, vol. 81, no. 1, 2011, pp. 14–23, https://doi.org/10.1002/ad.1184.

10 Henry, Todd A. *Assimilating Seoul: Japanese Rule and the Politics of Public Space in Colonial Korea, 1910–1945*. Berkeley: University of California Press, 2016, p. 23.

11 "Seoul – 2.3 Population Changes in Hanseong." *Seoul – 2.3 Population Changes in Hanseong – CefiaWiki*, 19 Jan. 2017, http://cefia.aks.ac.kr:84/index.php?title=Seoul_-_2.3_Population_Changes_in_Hanseong.

12 Kim, Mun Taek, editor. *Seoul Museum of History: Places and Memories*. Seoul: Seoul Museum of History, 2013, pp. 112–115.

13 Kim, Mun Taek, editor. *Seoul Museum of History: Places and Memories*. Seoul: Seoul Museum of History, 2013, p. 112.

14 "Seoul – 4.1 Population Growth and Expansion of the Urban Center." *Seoul – 4.1 Population Growth and Expansion of the Urban Center – CefiaWiki*, 19 Jan. 2017, http://cefia.aks.ac.kr:84/index.php?title=Seoul_-_4.1_Population_Growth_and_Expansion_of_the_Urban_Center.

15 Henry, Todd A. *Assimilating Seoul: Japanese Rule and the Politics of Public Space in Colonial Korea, 1910–1945*. Berkeley: University of California Press, 2016, p. 28.

16 Kim, Mun Taek, editor. *Seoul Museum of History: Places and Memories*. Seoul: Seoul Museum of History, 2013, p. 226.

17 Graham, Edward M. "The Miracle with a Dark Side: Korean Economic Development Under Park Chung Hee." *Reforming Korea's Industrial Conglomerates*. Washington, DC: Peterson Institute for International Economics, 2003, pp. 11–24.

18 Ibid.

19 Kim, Joochul, and Ch'oe Sang-ch'ŏl. *Seoul: The Making of a Metropolis*. London: Wiley, 1997.

20 Kim, Kwang-jung. *Seoul, Twentieth Century, Growth and Change of the Last 100 Years*. Seoul: Seoul Development Institute, 2003, p. 127.

21 Seoul Solution. "Sewun Mall Development Plan." 서울정책아카이브 *Seoul Solution*, 25 Sept. 2017, https://seoulsolution.kr/en/node/6304.

22 Seoul Solution. "Development of Gangnam." 서울정책아카이브 *Seoul Solution*, 12 Dec. 2017, www.seoulsolution.kr/en/node/3445.

23 Yun, Jieheerah. *Globalizing Seoul: The City's Cultural and Urban Change*. Abingdon, Oxfordshire: Routledge, Taylor & Francis Group, 2018, p. 1.

24 Ibid., p. 3.

25 *European Capitals of Culture – European Commission*. https://ec.europa.eu/culture/sites/default/files/capitals-culture-candidates-guide_en_vdec17.pdf.

26 Koolhaas, Rem. "The City of the Captive Globe." *The City of the Captive Globe*, 1 Jan. 1972, https://dome.mit.edu/handle/1721.3/21258.
27 Seoul Solution. "1. Cheonggyecheon (Stream) Restoration." 서울정책아카이브 *Seoul Solution*, 28 Sept. 2017, www.seoulsolution.kr/en/content/7475.
28 Yun, Jieheerah. *Globalizing Seoul: The City's Cultural and Urban Change*. Abingdon, Oxfordshire: Routledge, Taylor & Francis Group, 2018, p. 109.
29 "Seoullo 7017 Skygarden." *MVRDV*, www.mvrdv.nl/projects/208/seoullo-7017-skygarden.
30 Architecture, Dominique Perrault. "Dominique Perrault Architecture." *Dominique Perrault Architecture – LIGHTWALK – Gangnam Intermodal Transit Center, Seoul*, www.perraultarchitecture.com/en/projects/3463-lightwalk_-_gangnam_intermodal_transit_center_seoul.html.
31 Seoul Solution. "[Inclusive Growth] Sharing City Seoul Project." 서울정책아카이브 *Seoul Solution*, 28 June 2017, https://seoulsolution.kr/en/content/inclusive-growth-sharing-city-seoul-project.
32 Doxiadis, C. A., and J. G. Papaioannou. *Ecumenopolis: The Inevitable City of the Future*. New York: Norton, 1975.
33 Cronon, William. "The Trouble with Wilderness: Or, Getting Back to the Wrong Nature." *Environmental History*, vol. 1, no. 1, Jan. 1996, pp. 7–28. Published by: Forest History Society and American Society for Environmental History.
34 Neil Brenner expands on the idea that planetary urbanism is still simply the project of urbanization and should not be labeled otherwise. Brenner, Neil. "Debating Planetary Urbanization: For an Engaged Pluralism." *Environment and Planning D: Society and Space*, vol. 36, no. 3, 2018, pp. 570–590, https://doi.org/10.1177/0263775818757510.
35 Bratton, Benjamin H. *The Stack – on Software and Sovereignty*. Cambridge, MA: MIT Press, 2016.
36 Bekaert, Geert, et al. *After-Sprawl: Research for the Contemporary City*. Edited by Xaveer De Geyter. Rotterdam: NAi Publishers, 2002.
37 Ungers, O. M., et al. *The City in the City: Berlin: A Green Archipelago*. Zurich: Lars Müller Publishers, 2013.
38 Allen, Stan. *Points + Lines: Diagrams and Projects for the City*. New York: Princeton Architectural Press, 2012.
39 Waldheim, Charles. *The Landscape Urbanism Reader*. New York: Princeton Architectural Press, 2006.
   Waldheim, Charles. *Landscape as Urbanism a General Theory*. New York: Princeton University Press, 2016.
40 Hilberseimer, Ludwig, et al. *Metropolisarchitecture and Selected Essays*. New York: GSAPP Books, 2012.
41 Rossi, Aldo. *The Architecture of the City*. Cambridge, MA: MIT Press, 2007, p. 21.
42 Frampton, Adam, et al. *Cities Without Ground: A Hong Kong Guidebook*. Navato, CA: Oro Editions, 2012.
43 Kaijima, Momoyo, et al. *Made in Tokyo*. Tokyo: Kajima Institute Publishing Co., Ltd., 2021.

2 A History of Infra-Architecture

The works of Ahn Sekwon in his triptych series (Lights of Wolgok-dong, 2005; Disappearing Lights of Wolgok-dong I, 2006; and Disappearing Lights of Wolgok-dong II, 2007) depict the rapid pace in which Seoul's urban scene changes, eradicating entire neighborhoods deemed as slums in order to make way for new developments. The photographs offer a comparison of the before and after conditions, showing a brightly lit single-story neighborhood in 2005 and the remaining debris from the demolition in 2007. The later photograph highlights in sharp contrast a well-lit road as the only remnant of the previous condition after the neighborhood is demolished. Despite this being an informal settlement, the infrastructural path dependency is clearly shown through the remains of this road portraying infrastructure as a leading factor in the organization of the settlement with no real recognition for what the role of architecture is in this condition. The roads remain while the interior of the block can change from a dilapidated condition to new building construction without changing the block logic or its infrastructure.

This process of redevelopment demonstrates the domineering role infrastructure has taken in the expansion of the urbanized world. For architecture to take a part in the process, it must evaluate infrastructure as a hybrid architectural condition. In order to reframe architecture as a tool for urbanization, rather than focus on a pure infrastructural organization, this chapter focuses on the emergence of the infra-architectural hybrid after the project of urbanization was introduced by Ildefons Cerdà in 1867.

Cerdà's General Theory of Urbanization serves as the perfect starting point for investigating infra-architectural hybrids, as Cerdà introduces the project of urbanization as a distinct phenomenon to which "city" was no longer an applicable term.

> Sabe que el conjunto de todas estas cosas, sobre todo en su parte material, se llama ciudad; mas como mi objeto no era expresar esa materialidad, si más bien la manera y sistema que siguen esos grupos al formarse, y cómo están organizados y funcionan después todos los elementos que los constituyen, es decir, que además de la materialidad debía expresar

DOI: 10.4324/9781032684963-2

el organismo, la vida si así cabe decirlo, que anima a la parte material; es claro y evidente, que aquella palabra no podía convenirme.[1]

The set of all these things, especially in their material part, is called a city; but since my object was not to express that materiality, but rather the way and system that these groups follow when they are formed, and how all the elements that constitute them are organized and function afterwards, that is, that in addition to the materiality I had to express the organism, life if it is possible to say so, that animates the material part; it is clear and evident that that word could not suit me.[2]

The concrete notion that "city" was different from what was needed to describe what he calls a *mare-magnum* of people led him to appropriate the term "Urbs" from the Romans, a term they used to demarcate an area of population. Cerdà mentions as well his preference for "population" rather than "citizens," which was a term also used by the Romans and derived from the Latin *civitas*. Citizen reflects more on a social construct rather than the material context. Terminologies like village, town, or city also have a hierarchical connotation based on size, while Cerdà considered the Latin Urbs to be nonhierarchical. This nonhierarchical condition is a key element for forming a science with principles, doctrines, and rules for collective edifications, their groupings, and the way they foment development and the welfare of individuals and the public. This science was termed "urbanization."

conjunto de principios, doctrinas y reglas que deben aplicarse para que la edificación y su agrupamiento . . . sirvan para fomentar su desarrollo y vigor y bienestar individual y felicidad pública.[3]

set of principles, doctrines and rules that must be applied so that the building and its grouping . . . serve to promote its development and vigor and individual well-being and public happiness.[4]

In the General Theory of Urbanization, Cerdà describes urbanization starting as a relationship between housing and its role for socialization (*sociabilidad*). In order to produce a beneficial socialization, urbanization must then be understood as a science that would rely on the quantitative measures of statistics for an infrastructural layout with the purpose of allowing industry, public health, sociability, well-being, and development of the city to occur. The *Eixample*, a gridded expansion for Barcelona, would serve as a test for proposing a composition of overlaid infrastructures, both hard and soft, organized by the grid for the purpose of producing a new social order in a calculated manner.

These criteria were aimed at the homogeneous and controllable redistribution of social wealth, and made clear at the scale of urban design a method of governance in which social wealth and economic control of the working class – and thus the security of urban space – were at stake. For this Cerdà drafted an isotropic grid of 133-by-133-meter blocks, which articulated the equal distribution of services and roads throughout the city area. A religious center appeared in every nine-block district, a marketplace every four blocks, a park every eight, a hospital every sixteen. These were distributed according to a density of 250 inhabitants per hectare, the standard recommended to guarantee a maximum hygienic social order.[5]

As a result, urbanization under the framework of Cerdà, is an infrastructural process that allows for an equitable distribution of services and amenities through a nonhierarchical grid.

Industry and Mobility

An emerging industrial revolution at the end of the 19th century and beginning of the 20th century would foment the need for an urban expansion as cities became overcrowded and polluted. Industry gradually would be pushed to the fringe areas as larger facilities were needed, and the labor force would move with it, away from the city center. This phenomenon produced a capitalist disparity that was addressed with other urban models such as the Garden City movement[6] in the United Kingdom (1898), by Ebenezar Howard, and the *Cité Industrielle*[7] in France (1904), by Tony Garnier. Garden City aimed at becoming an alternative for the growing working class by providing self-sufficient agrarian towns of 32,000 people. This anti-capitalist model would be organized through radial farming enclaves that separated agricultural zones, residential zones, and industrial zones. These would form concentrically around a larger city center. Tony Garnier focused on the concentration of industry within the city in a model that separated work, housing, health, and leisure with his project of the *Cité Industrielle*, not published until 1917. This separation of zones would produce typologies based on the use case of the zone.

These early models revealed a new agenda for the modern city based on the relationship between industry and mobility: industry as the generator of capital, and mobility as access to labor in relation to dwellings. This posed the challenge of solving industrial and housing typologies as an architectural problem and mobility as an infrastructural one. An early theoretical proposal by Ludwig Hilberseimer sought to address this issue perhaps with the first example of an infra-architectural model.

In his book *Großstadt Architektur*,[8] Hilberseimer presents the case for a reconfiguration of infrastructure through an architectural urbanism, which he labels as the "Vertical City" for Berlin. This is in reflection to Le Corbusier's proposal for Paris, published two years earlier in 1925.

"Hilberseimer would have compared his book to Le Corbusier's 'Urbanisme (The City of Tomorrow and Its Planning)', 1925, the contents of which influenced significant elements of his own thinking."[9] In his book,

Hilberseimer analyzed in detail the proposal by Le Corbusier that led him to reflect on its validity and eventually led him to propose a new model.

Hilberseimer begins by reflecting on the new state of urbanity labeled as a metropolis. The metropolis is not necessarily derived from having a large population but as a modern condition driven by capitalism and an internationalism unlike the previous royal city model.

> Thus the present form of the metropolis owes its appearance primarily to the economic form of capitalist imperialism, which, for its part, developed in close collaboration with science and technologies of production . . . many overlooked the fact that the metropolis itself accelerates economic production processes by drawing economic control ever faster and more consciously to itself.[10]

Capitalism, for Hilberseimer, requires certain elements of density in order to optimize the productive workforce within the city. New models of cities like the radial and linear models become difficult to manage as the city expands due to the larger territory infrastructure needs to cover. The skyscraper American model offers density as an interior condition through its building typology but is flawed as an exterior experience. Hilberseimer explains that while a single building can house a larger workforce, the sidewalks needed to support such a density would produce incredibly wide streets and hinder pedestrian and vehicular traffic. Le Corbusier's conceptual proposal for a "City of Three Million Inhabitants" is used by Hilberseimer instead as an analytical starting point for solving the chaos of the metropolis. Le Corbusier's proposal focused on a hypothetical flat terrain that would be subdivided into three regions: urban, suburban, and mixed. The city center is composed of 60-story high-rises with a building coverage ratio of 5% allowing for parks and recreation facilities in between to ease the high density of the towers. From the city center employees, 400,000–600,000 workers are meant to live in the residential district bordering the center, while 2 million people live in the suburban garden city in dwellings of 100 m^2. The generous transport system is meant to alleviate the illness of the metropolitan traffic with ample streets, subway system, bus lanes, elevated highways, and trains that connect commuters to the central core. While at first, Hilberseimer praises the qualitative state of the plan, he questions its quantitative measures. The density that Le Corbusier claims to achieve is entirely based on building typologies that have been based on zoning. Yet, according to Hilberseimer, residential densities cannot be compared to commercial densities. The demands for street space that the high-rises would require would also use the open space.

> Thus if each person is allotted an average of three-four square meters of street space, that comes to a total circulation area of 75,000 to 100,000 square meters. This spatial requirement causes the park and green spaces

to shrink to such an extent that only two to three square meters are left per person.[11]

Hilberseimer claims that the same density can be achieved by buildings of five stories. He concludes that Le Corbusier's solution is merely an aesthetic one that orders the city through a geometric rigor but fails to address the core issue. "The traffic problem will not be solved by increasing the means of transportation but by radically eliminating the need of traffic."[12] In short, Le Corbusier's plan focuses on a geometric composition that uses specific typologies in relation to a horizontal zoning relationship between living and working.

Hilberseimer introduced a different attitude toward urbanization through a hybrid typology that responded to the new mobile mechanized urban life as a stacking of two cities: the working city and the living city. Unlike the horizontal separation of zones by Le Corbusier, Hilberseimer's hypothetical reconstruction for Berlin demonstrated the systematization and the reproductivity of a typology in order to produce an urbanization effect by vertically stacking programs in order to produce each block as a micro-city. Each block would be composed of a podium that would hold offices and productive spaces and an elevated pedestrian network that would meet a residential block on top of the podium. The car would remain at ground level in order to separate pedestrians from vehicles as a solution to traffic. The housing blocks would consist of hotel typologies as the new mobile life would allow residents to work and live anywhere along this infinite grid. The most important part of this theoretical project was the fact that the building block could be infinitely reproduced forming the urbanized grid. Architecture became a systematic prototype that directly confronted the realities of the new found personalized mobility. Each city block was architecture as well as infrastructure, repeatable in a grid pattern.

Decentralization

As urbanization gave way to the expansion of cities, industry would begin to disperse in fringe areas through zoning regulations as manifested by the La Sarraz Declaration and the Charter of Athens.[13] The newly formed Congrès Internationaux d'Architecture Moderne (CIAM) theorized the modern city as separated by functions and accessible through the modern forms of transportation such as the private vehicle and trains. Cities were becoming decentralized through the suburbanization process, displacement of industry, improvements to personal mobility, and advances in communication technology. In the American context, project manifestos like "Broadacre City,"[14] Frank Lloyd Wright disregarded the idea of the city as a concentrated settlement by proposing a dispersal or diffusion of the city into the landscape by means of technology: the car allowed for mobility; the radio, the telephone, and the telegraph facilitated communication; and standardized machine-shop production.[15] The premise of this conceptual project is that each household would receive one acre of land for agricultural production. In this case, industry or production is decentralized to the level of the individual. Although originally introduced in 1932, Broadacre City was not popularized as a manifesto until it was exhibited at the MoMA as an antithesis to New York City in 1935.[16] The introduction of new telecommunications infrastructure and the possibility of new transportation technology would completely revolutionize the concept of the city into an early model of a decentralized infrastructural network.

The process of decentralizing the city became a major concern for Josep Lluis Sert during his tenure as the president of the CIAM (1947–1956).

I dread the pictures of the "city of tomorrow" which appear frequently in popular magazines, a "city" formed of endless suburbs; one small cottage next to the next one and a helicopter in every backyard! . . . suburban trends seem to be favored and little or nothing new is suggested when it comes to the real problem areas or those nearer the center of our cities.[17]

Proceeding the CIAM 8 (The Heart of the City), Sert emphasized the need for a new civic core as an architectural project that would revitalize the city and produce a new ordering system. Sert's essay on "Centres of Community Life" requests a reevaluation at the dispersion effect and a thinning out of the city centers caused by suburbanization.[18] His vision of a modern Agora romanticizes a nostalgia of a pre-machine era where citizens could group around civic places. These can be modernized through architecture, planning technology, and art by producing community centers depending on the urban scales followed by one larger civic center that would become the core of the city.

These cores will act as catalyzing elements, so that around them the life of the community will develop. In these new nuclei, public buildings of different types will be grouped in harmony of form and space; they will be the meeting places of the people, community centres where the pedestrians will be given preference over traffic and business interest.[19]

In a span of a decade, Sert proposed a series of masterplans in Latin America that focused on the civic core as the primary architectural component that organized the city. Some of the more significant unrealized projects like the Cidad do Motores (1945), Plan for Bogota (1951–1953), Plan of Chimbote (1948), Plan for Medellin (1949), and Plan for Havana (1955–1958) proposed large pedestrian zones that would be framed with monumental architecture.

By comparing these examples from Sert, some key points stand out with respect to the infra-architectural hybrid. First, Sert's preoccupation with centralization had the effect of monumentality in scale. All these projects would take over several city blocks with a singular architectural project. Despite

Sert calling for urban design and city planning, his projects focus on the architectural intervention at the scale of infrastructure. Second, in order to produce a pedestrian zone, a pedestrian infrastructure was created separately from the vehicular one, and it was integral to the architecture. This was done through podiums, decks, plazas, and arcades that would extend from the architecture.

One year after the CIAM 8 (The Heart of the City) was held, the idea for a new decentralized democratic system emerged through the Golden Lane competition held in 1952. This competition aimed at redeveloping the East End of London, which was still heavily damaged from the war. Alison and Peter Smithsons' entry (not the winning proposal) introduces the concept of a "street in the air" in order to produce a vibrant interconnectedness through an upper gallery that would link slab buildings.[20] This would allow residents to have extended social spaces no matter the vertical level. "The idea of designing a gallery as if it were a street is born of the wish to integrate the residential building into the city's socio-cultural fabric."[21] Heuvel claims that the "street in the air" sparks from two examples that would guide the Smithsons: Michiel Brinkman's Spangen Quarter Housing from 1919 and Le Corbusier's *Unité d'Habitation* de Marseille completed in 1952. The Spangen Quarter Housing offered an internal block system for the upper galleries where residents could sit outside and children could play while facing the inner courtyard. The *Unité d'Habitation* would introduce the *rue intérieure* into his building, accessible through a central gallery with the same aim. Heuvel points out that the Smithsons moved the gallery to the facade in order to engage the public, perhaps as an evolution from the precedents.

While both represented a decentralized idea of urbanization, there is a much larger distinction to be made at the urban model level; Le Corbusier's *Unité d'Habitation* worked as a repeatable urban island unit,[22] while Golden Lane developed an idea for a connected megastructural network.[23] The *Unité d'Habitation* was in essence a self-contained micro-city, as quoted by Sbriglio, "un nouvel ordre de grandeur des éléments urbains," translated as, "a new order of grandeur of urban elements."[24] The *rue intérieure*, which ran on every third floor, was a representation of the street that offers a common promenade. This autonomous model could be repeated as a unit once there was a need for new housing and in fact was copied as the *Unité d'Habitation* of Nantes-Rezé in 1955, *Unité d'Habitation* of Berlin in 1957, *Unité d'Habitation* of Briey in 1963, and *Unité d'Habitation* of Firminy-Vert in 1965 – all as autonomous separate buildings.[25] On the other hand, while the Golden Lane competition entry from 1952 would focus on the Golden Lane Estate located on the intersection between Golden Lane and Fann Street in London's East End (see figure 35), it would evolve as an urbanization model through the expansion of connected elevated decks, presented during the CIAM IX in Aix-en-Provence, France, on July 1953.

CIAM IX was characterized as the largest CIAM congress up to date with over 3,000 delegates, members, and observers, a large portion of whom would represent the younger critical voice for a new urban agenda.[26] Among the participants, aside from the Smithsons, were Aldo van Eyck, Jaap Bakema, Georges Candilis, and Shadrach Woods. During this conference, the Smithsons showcased a radical evolution for Golden Lane accompanied with the theoretical text "Urban Re-Identification."[27] Golden Lane would not be shown as a parcelized building condition but as a connected dispersal; a branching housing project that formed its own pedestrian network above the modernist vehicular grid as an overimposition. It would challenge replacing the modern functionalism of dwelling, work, recreation, and transportation with a "hierarchy of associational elements"[28] expressed as house, street, district, and city. The branching form of this proposal would evaluate the relationship between the house and the different scales represented by the deck as the street, a branch as a district, and the overall megaform as the city. Hence, it perhaps introduces an initial notion of a megastructure for urbanization.

"Golden Lane is a piece of connective urban form of sufficient size to match in scale those last pieces of urban-form invention, the railway stations that followed directly on from Stephenson's invention of the railway engine."[29]

Following the disbandment of the CIAM and the formation of Team X, a new agenda was introduced through an infrastructural and systematic approach to architecture that gave rise to movements for studying the potential for megastructures, such as the Situationist, Structuralism, and Metabolism. These were projects that were dealing with the reconstruction of cities, an opposition to Modernist functionalism, and a new agenda for future cities. The megaform and megastructure project became highly critical during an age of urban development in the decades of the sixties and seventies, as they manifested a physical representation of the imminent infrastructural growth that was yet to come from the increasing vehicular demands. The Team X primer released in 1962 would call for a development of "road and communication systems as the urban infrastructure. (Motorways as a unifying force). And to realize the implications of flow and movement in the architecture itself."[30] These projects were meant to represent the idealization of typologies that hybridized transportation infrastructure with urban fabric for the purpose of optimizing the land. They sought to resolve the city as a three-dimensional space where architecture and infrastructure intertwined. These are projects that identify mobility infrastructure as the spatial generator for the city and could be used as an architectural compositional instrument for generating urbanism.

As expressed by the Smithsons, this hybrid process for understanding the relationships between the street life and the building aimed at investigating social relationships and social constructs.[31] This theme aligned with the evolving explorations of Structuralism, informed by the writings of Claude Lévi-Strauss. Strauss would form the basis of Structuralist theories in anthropology, focusing on understanding the underlying patterns of human thinking and semiology,[32] which were later expanded by Lacan, Barthes, and Foucault on issues of the signified and signifier. The newly found studies on semiology heavily influenced architects such as Aldo van Eyck and Herman Hertzberger in what would become Dutch Structuralism during the 1960s and 1970s. Hertzberger interprets the studies in semiology (including that of Saussure) as translatable to an architecture that requires an underlying structure that allows for mutations while maintaining its characteristic qualities. "The relation between a collective given and individual interpretation as it exists between form and usage as well as the experience thereof may be compared to the relation between language and speech."[33] Program is not a defining formal element, instead the underlying structure allows for adaptability based on its users, just like language forms the structure for colloquial speech. Hertzberger's Central Beheer office building in Apeldoorn (1968) explores this condition through an aggregation of identical spatial modules that connect to form inner "street" circulation with non-specific usage of space.

Architectural historian Lisbeth Söderqvist argues that Structuralism influenced architecture through the logic of binary constructs, particularly that of the inside versus the outside.[34] In the proposals from Candilis, Josic, and Woods for Römerberg, Frankfurt am Main (1963), as well as the Freie Universität Berlin from the same year, the binary relationship between inside and outside through streets and buildings formed urban structures rather than a collection of buildings. Analogous to streets forming blocks to which buildings would infill, these proposals internalized the streets as a gridded built form that would allow for adaptable infills to be built as needed over time. As expressed by Hertzberger who discussed the project with Shadrach Woods,

> This project may well be the very first true structuralist concept; an unchanging, extendable structure that can accept and enable local changes in infill and indicates a distinction between what in principle is a guiding and immutable structure and the variable and varied infill which, compared with the structure, operates to a short time cycle.[35]

In the American context, contemporary to the Structuralist projects of Candilis, Josic, and Woods, Paul Rudolph initiated a study for the Lower Manhattan Expressway (LOMEX) in 1967, funded by the Ford Foundation.[36] LOMEX had been projected in the 1940s by Robert Moses as a slum clearing project that would connect the Manhattan Bridge and Williamsburg Bridge in the East River to the Holland Tunnel in the Hudson River.[37] Ultimately, Moses's project was scrapped after opposition from the local neighborhood.

> In 1961, residents of Greenwich Village, including Jacobs, formed the Committee to Save the West Village to halt the construction of the Lower

Manhattan Expressway. Their efforts not only stopped this project, but also brought the power structure of Moses's New York to an end.[38]

Through the Ford Foundation Grant, Rudolph envisioned a masterplan for the Lower Manhattan Area entitled "New Forms of the Evolving City,"[39] where a megastructure spanned the width of Lower Manhattan, camouflaging the expressway with a continuous strip of housing that would cluster or straddle the infrastructure. From Rudolph's renderings, there is an apparent similitude between this project and Metabolist projects with main structural frames and plug-in units. Yet, in an interview between Robert Bruegmann and Paul Rudolph at the Art Institute in Chicago from 1986, Rudolph tries to distance himself from the Metabolist. He explains that the apparent similarity is a causality of the scale of the project and not the intent. "In my project for the Lower Manhattan Expressway that was clearly a part of the thinking because it was so large that programmatically things would change."[40] He is talking about the possibility of programs and elements to change within the structural frame, which makes this project a linear megastructure.

Megastructure as Urban Scaffolding

Paper projects like Yona Friedman's "Ten Principles of Mobile Town Planning" from 1959[41] introduced a new strategy for reconfiguring the city as a three-dimensional space rather than a planar condition for the purpose of urban optimization. The ten principles were:

1 Leisure centers are the future of the city while other functions are automated.
2 The citizen must be freed from the wills of the urban planner.
3 Agriculture is needed inside the city.
4 The city must be acclimatized.
5 The buildings that form the city must conform to a technical scale.
6 The new city must be the intensification of the existing city.
7 Three-dimensional urbanism allows for an overlap of neighborhoods.
8 Building structures must be skeletons that can be filled as needed.
9 This model is for cities with over 3 million inhabitants.
10 The whole population of Europe can be concentrated in 120 of these cities.[42]

These principles are trying to combat the urban sprawl and the formation of megalopolis. Points 6–8 introduce the "Ville Spatiale," a space frame that spans over the air rights of the city, densifying the underutilized areas and urban voids. As an architectural solution, the "Ville Spatiale" allows for the city to operate as an open-ended volume, serving as a framework where programs can be plugged-in as needed. This also reinforces the idea of a dynamic, ever-changing city, perhaps spontaneous in nature rather than fully masterplanned, as hinted by point 2 and point 8 again.

Contemporary to Friedman, in 1957 the newly formed Situationist group released an abstract mapping project entitled "The Naked City." Attributed to Guy Debord, this map presented a new conception for reading the city through the appropriation of space. The map reconstructed Paris through a series of cutout plans from different neighborhoods like the Jardin du Luxembourg, Les Halles, Gare de Lyon, the Pantheon, among others.[43] As explained by Thomas McDonough, the map answered questions regarding the construction and perception of space framed under the guides of the Situationist.[44] The map was to be "figured as narratives rather than as tools of 'universal knowledge.'"[45] Debord questioned cartography and geography in the traditional sense for mapping space. The map can be interpreted instead as neighborhood islands that define the collective knowledge of Paris; destination enclaves on how the user moves throughout the city. "It is predicted on a model of moving, on 'spatializing actions', known to the Situationist as *dérives*; rather than presenting the city from a totalizing point of view, it organizes movements metaphorically around psychogeographic hubs."[46] As explained by Mark Wigley, Debord sought for a cultural revolution in the occupation of the city questioning the result of capitalist urbanism ("totalizing point of view" of a masterplan) where the spaces produced were those of alienation and constraint.[47]

This new conception of the city as a scaffolding of fluid situations based on the Situationist and Debord's Theory of the Dérive led to Constant's contribution to the development of New Babylon in 1960. This was to become a new setting for nomadic wandering. This anti-architectural statement called for settings where the nomad could alter the surroundings for the purpose of immediacy as a critical new apparatus that negated the constraints of the modern city and instead a self-designed city. The models displayed at the permanent collection from the Kunstmuseum Den Haag show the intent of producing a large temporary structure that would span over the city as a scaffolding. In Constant's words,

> New Babylon is a gigantic labyrinthine complex raised above the earth on tall pillars. All forms of transport circulate below it. The various tiers of the city can be reached via lifts and stairs and are almost entirely roofed-in and climate-controlled. With their many levels and terraces, they form a vast multi-layered space that constantly offers new surprises as a result of its functional flexibility, climatic variability and light and sound effects. New Babylonians can wander around like modern nomads, in search of new experiences and unknown sensations.[48]

Constant was intrigued by the settings of migration that allowed for this break from the modern stasis and placed the wanderer into a new confluence of situations and events.

Constant preceded to contrast this sedentary image of urban life with what he saw as its antithesis: the promise of a new nomadic lifestyle in buildings having to do with "departures and arrivals," buildings such as train stations, harbors, and, above all else, airports.[49]

These infrastructural components were to become the new catalyst for an active city. New Babylon, although read as a megastructure spanning over the city, was meant to imply a temporality, a fourth dimension of time.

Metabolism

While megaforms, megastructures, and Structuralism had predominantly emerged from the need to reconstruct Europe with new urban models, World War II had also made a lasting impact in Japan with the unprecedented release of two nuclear bombs by the United States that obliterated Hiroshima and Nagasaki. Added to natural disasters that have continuously threatened Japanese cities, a narrative was formed for Metabolism starting in 1960 as a new form of avant-garde architecture out of the post-war Tabula Rasa condition. This can be seen in its theoretical roots, which originated from the Tange Lab at Tokyo University, where Kenzo Tange was commissioned to study the master planning of the war-torn cities in Japan.

> When we saw our national land turned into scorched earth in which nothing remained but a sparse scattering of burnt concrete structures, we had a dream and hope of drawing a new city as if on a blank white sheet. But we soon learned that there is a thick opaque layer of political, economic, and social realities beneath the scorched earth of each city.[50]

Eventually this impactful research would incite Metabolism to reflect on conditions for artificial ground.

Through a series of projects after his research on Hiroshima, Tange gained international notoriety and was invited to the 1959 CIAM XI in Otterlo, the Netherlands. Tange introduced the work of Kiyomori Kikutake, The Tower Shaped City, and the Sky House, framing a new attitude toward architects as city builders or architecture that could engage the organization and growth of the city. This focus guided Tange to push for this specific architectural agenda to be internationally exposed and grounded using the World Design Conference (WoDeCo) to be held the following year (1960) in Tokyo. That same year, Tange was also invited to teach at MIT and assigned Asada from the Tange Lab to scout for young talent in Japan in preparation for WoDeCo. While at MIT, Tange was able to explore the framework of what would become the Metabolism movement through the works of his students, proposing a housing complex for 25,000 people on the Boston Harbor. This would evolve into the famously published Tokyo Bay Project presented later at the WoDeCo. Upon his return for WoDeCo, the Metabolist Manifesto was published with four essays: Kikutake's "Ocean City," Kurokawa's "Space City,"

Maki and Otaka's "On Group Form," and Kawazoe's essay "I Want to Be a Sea-Shell, I Want to Be a Mold, I Want to Be a Spirit." As Rem Koolhaas theorizes in *Project Japan: Metabolism Talks . . .*, Japan had an awakening by architects in the wake of the post (atomic) war. Japan, like the West, was rebuilding, yet its population density and limited land led to alternative scenarios for using the sky and seas. Architecture could enter an era of city building and projects that followed the megastructural ordeal were repositioned to be incremental and adaptable. This was analogous to metabolism in biology, a city that can grow according to its needs.

The WoDeCo was able to formalize a group of architects under the Metabolism agenda: Kenzo Tange, Arata Isozaki, Kenji Ekuan, Kiyonori Kikutake, Kisho Kurokawa, Masato Otaka, Kiyoshi Awazu, Fumihiko Maki, and Noboru Kawazoe. Their manifesto *Metabolism: The Proposals for New Urbanism* would cement their common goal in exploring the growth of Japanese cities as an incremental flexible architecture.

> "Metabolism" is the name of the group, in which each member proposes future designs of our coming world through his concrete designs and illustrations. We regard human society as a vital process – a continuous development from atom to nebula. The reason why we use such a biological word, metabolism, is that we believe design and technology should be a denotation of human vitality.[51]

Following WoDeCo, these architects embarked in a series of explorations both built and unbuilt that generated a common body of work and a taxonomy of elements for metabolism that included the plug-in pod unit, artificial ground, infrastructural cores, and expansive space frames.

The pod is perhaps the most significant component within the Metabolism movement. Kurokawa declared, "The capsule stands for an emancipation of the building in relation to the ground and heralds the era of moving architecture."[52] Based on studies on prefabrication, the pod or capsule allows for programmatic functions to exist in individual containers, therefore allowing for diversity to exist three dimensionally in the city, but at the same time requiring some infrastructural network of services to plug into. Explorations on massive cores and space frames would address this issue. Hence, Metabolism relies on this duality between plug-in units (which can vary in scale) and infrastructure to hold them. The concept was presented at a large scale during the 1970s World Expo, where Tange features a 292 m × 108 m space frame canopy hovering 30 m up in the air. Awazu and Kurokawa designed capsules that plug into the canopy, which presented another theoretical implication for Metabolism to allow a multiplicity of elements to plug in simultaneously, regardless of the author.

While the majority of the Metabolism focused on the plug-in condition that evolved through megastructures, Maki would produce his own theories of an organic formal collective, largely based on his travels through the Middle East, Europe, and Asia. Awarded by the Graham Foundation, Maki was able to embark on a self-driven study of vernacular urban forms, which led him to write *Investigations on Collective Form*. Here a paradigm shift is suggested from theories of the individual form to an analysis of collective forms that shape our cities with an element of time.[53] He suggests that cities need to cope with the changing modern scales of mega highways and the disparate form of the city. Architects have adopted a sense of trying to achieve a unique building that outdoes the previous one, generating an eclectic cityscape with not much of an urban composition. For that reason, there should be an analytical study of the collective form that could restore a formal order to the city. Maki suggests that there are three approaches to the collective form theory made up of the compositional form, the megaform, and group form.

The compositional form is predetermined by the designer as a collection of building components. "It is a static approach, because the act of making a composition itself has a tendency to complete a formal statement."[54]

The megaform or megastructure is described as a large framework that houses all the components of the city. It is inherently static, and it tends to concentrate functions. Maki's criticism deals with the megaform's inability to deal with the rapid change of technology through time and might become obsolete. Instead, the megaform should work like a megastructure that can expand or contract offering flexibility of change. Its best potential attributes are for environmental engineering, multi-functional structures, and infrastructure as public investment.

The group form is described as the newest conceptual strategy for the collective form. "It is form which evolves from a system of generative elements in space."[55] Unlike the megaform, which Maki describes as needing a skeleton to frame growth, the group form is a system of elements that follow a code, resulting in an overall form that evolves in time. Maki shows the Japanese linear village, a medieval city, or a Greek mountain village as examples of group forms. The individual element has an inherent rule that allows its attachment to the system.

Performative Landscapes

Toward the end of the 20th century, there was a period of reflection on the process that had transpired since the inception of the project of urbanization. Essays such as "Bigness, or the Problem of Large"[56] and the "Generic City"[57] by Koolhaas from 1995 depicted the banal condition of cities that the project of urbanization had created. The "Generic City" described the process by which the repetitive process of development had been copied and modified across the globe generating a familiarity in the construct of the city, which was no longer contested as a form but as an endless urban field propagated by the urban grid. "Bigness" described the scale jump in architecture that had also generated a new relationship of large objects in the city. These big projects like the Euralille by OMA (1989–1994) produced an architecture of exterior shells that challenged the architectural process through the overscaled production of space. Euralille, for example, contained over 800,000 m² of offices, housing, commercial space, concert hall, and a new Trains à Grande Vitesse (TGV) station among others. At this scale, architecture competes with the scale of infrastructure as it only serves as a platform for programs and events to be plugged in independently from the shell.

At the same time that cities are being described as increasingly more ge-neric in makeup, new statistical and analytical technologies allowed for cities to be understood as a data set instead of through form. The development of the digitization process at the turn of the century would allow for large amounts of data to be collected at an unprecedented rate. For cities, this meant a new understanding in the way that cities can be managed through patterns of use rather than through form. Books such as the *Metropolitan World Atlas*[58] from 2005 by Arjen van Susteren or the 2007 book *The Endless City*[59] by the Lon-don School of Economics pointed out a new quantitative way for understand-ing and comparing cities through the visualization of statistical data rather than architecture or infrastructure. The collection of data became imperative for the function of these vast urban landscapes giving rise to the phenomena of "smart cities." As explained by Antoine Picon, large cities would operate through control rooms that could monitor the city through screens in order to manage a response in real time.[60]

Regardless of the newly adopted smart infrastructure that would serve to better manage the legacy infrastructure, formless urbanism kept on expand-ing at vast scales. This resulted in a series of architectural studies that engage issues of city form through expansive formal infrastructures focusing on the manipulation of hybrid conditions for the sake of urban optimization.

Through his 1999 book *Points + Lines: Diagrams and Projects for the City*,[61] Stan Allen makes the claim that architects can begin to redirect their own imaginative and technical efforts toward questions of infrastructure. This will allow for the profession to engage territorial organization and functionality. Practice should shift toward infrastructure. "Going beyond stylistic or formal issues, infrastructural urbanism offers a new model for practice and a renewed sense of architecture's potential to structure the future of the city."[62] Architec-ture should not be about surfaces and images as the postmodernists suggested but should refocus as a material practice that proposes strategies for working with large scales of performance in time rather than symbolic imagery. By en-gaging architecture as an infrastructural urbanism, architecture can condition the ground for future unforeseen events, managing complex systems that can adapt through time. Infrastructural urbanism opened the possibilities to engage the city as an architectural project rather than an urbanization project providing a new growth logic. The theory was further developed as a collection of essays from various practitioners in 2006 and presented as the *Landscape Urban-ism Reader*[63] edited by Charles Waldheim. Landscape Urbanism proposes the use of landscapes as an infrastructural operative field by which a city can be organized. A decade later, *Landscape as Urbanism: A General Theory*[64] was published by Waldheim, reflecting on a decade of theory being put into practice through the implementation of master plans from James Corner, West 8, among other landscape firms encroaching on the role of city planners.

In highly dense cities like Hong Kong, Tokyo, and Seoul, where real estate demands an optimization of use, these infrastructural hybrids can be more easily found through the blurring of private and public space. In 2012, Adam Frampton, Jonathan D. Solomon, and Clara Wong published a research mapping the pedestrian levels and connections of Hong Kong. *Cities Without Ground: A Hong Kong Guidebook*[65] demonstrated the three dimensionality of Hong Kong, which operates as a seamless continuity of a pedestrian infrastructural network of bridges and tunnels that pass through private blocks at various levels. These are formed through the overimposition of infrastructure onto the private sector. This presents the case for the infrastructural space to act as the commons for a city with lack of space.

Similarly to the condition already explained in *Cities Without Ground* in Hong Kong, the works of Weiss Manfredi published in 2015 as *Public Natures: Evolutionary Infrastructures*[66] radically proposes the merger between the public infrastructural space and the private programmatic space as new typologies that allow that duplicity in use, as seen through their works primarily in an American context. Referencing Landscape Urbanism, they propose an infrastructural architecture that allows the growth of the city to occur at a gradual organic pace, integrating evolutionary ecology as seen in their Seattle Olympic Park.

A Recap for Seoul

The general condensation of this historical background reveals specific instances where architecture and infrastructure have had a clear grafting or nondistinction for the purpose of defining a city form or an urban framework. Although most of the projects from the 1960s (megastructures, Situationist space frames, Metabolism, and Structuralist) sought to redevelop the city, they mainly remained as unbuilt visions. The few that got built became isolated typologies rather than urban systems. Some became barriers in the fabric when they were projected as singular megaforms, often resulting in abandonment such as the Brunswick in the 1980s in London. As Kenneth Frampton points in his 1986 essay, "The Generic Street as a Continuous Built Form,"[67] the initial preoccupation of the street as a social contextual urban form was unable to find a proper model of urbanization. This continuous struggle, Frampton suggests, has produced two questions.

First, in what way may megastructural forms, such as the freeway, be used to impart landmark identity to the large-scale megapolitan reality; and second, the related issue as to what may be an appropriate formulation for large urban elements such as mass housing, so that these will not only relate to the megapolitan scale but at the same time "situate" man and provide for those fundamental needs of association and identity.[68]

Frampton notes that this concept has been tested by protagonists like Team X, the Smithsons, and the Metabolists with Maki and Ohtaka, through a series of megastructural projects over a period of 20 years. These continuous studies have focused on two concerns: first, the technical viability with its experiential capability, and second, its limits and usefulness through an "open design" strategy. Louis Kahn's midtown Philadelphia project and the Smithsons' Haupstadt Berlin project are mentioned by Frampton as being the emblematic projects for this query. These projects fail in solving the important integration between vehicle and pedestrian networks though. The separation of both systems often ends in the vehicular circulation becoming the dominant element. This is not only a problem relating to the separation of networks but the failure to provide a theoretical model for a livable urban block that responds to the contemporary condition.

Furthermore, there seems to be a necessity to reintroduce into the abstract anonymity of the megapolis type forms, which are capable of generating something of that sense of public space or rather place that has always characterized the denser parts of the traditional city; to engender, as it were, breaks in the abstract motopian system, which are identifiable and sustainable as public enclaves of varying density and capacity.[69]

Despite the criticism from these avant-garde proposals, their value stands as projects that sought to structure city form or produce urbanity through architecture. They address issues of urban sprawl that remain as a contemporary concern, and their strategies could yield some contemporary solutions of megacities of the 21st century. Through the cross reference of the discussed projects, some common strategies are shared. They highlighted the need for infrastructural commons to be formalized as the guiding urban framework, the need for new pedestrian grounds, and the dichotomy between temporal and permanent. These are conditions that describe the way Seoul can be experienced and understood as an architectural formation and not a formless urban sprawl. As an urban framework, Seoul can be experienced through its subway system that connects the majority of its neighborhoods. One will move from Seongsu-dong to Hongdae using Line 2, uninterrupted from aboveground conditions, for example. This experience of being able to move around the 605 km^2 that make up Seoul and pop in and out of the subway system provides a seamless connection throughout the entire city, and this book argues that it is perhaps the primary organizational logic of the city. This underground system has evolved (mutated) not only as an infrastructural system of transportation but also as a pedestrian layer of the city – a new pedestrian ground that was theorized by the avant-garde perhaps. The city can be experienced underground as much as aboveground through underground markets, retail, production, educational, cultural, and civic spaces. Now, perhaps this dichotomy of aboveground versus underground and moving from one neighborhood to the other through the subway makes the neighborhoods feel autonomous from each other because of the physical distance, but this is comparable to the third point, the relationship between temporal and permanent. Neighborhoods, or better yet, city blocks, can be experienced autonomously, and they can drastically change over time, while the underground system remains as a permanent condition. This allows for the city to maintain a very dynamic and organized structure where the user, resident, and visitor can easily orient themselves in this massive city.

Notes

1 Cerdá Ildefonso. *Teoría General De La urbanización y aplicación De Sus Principios y Doctrinas a La Reforma y Ensanche De Barcelona*, vol. 1. Madrid: Imprenta Española, 1867, p. 29.
2 Ibid., p. 29 Translation.
3 Ibid., p. 30.
4 Ibid., p. 30 Translation.
5 Aureli, Pier Vittorio. *The Possibility of an Absolute Architecture*. Cambridge, MA: MIT Press, 2011, p. 10.
6 Howard, Ebenezer, et al. *Garden Cities of To-morrow*. Cambridge, MA: The MIT Press, 2007.
7 Garnier, Tony, and Riccardo Mariani. *Tony Garnier: Une Cite Industrielle*. New York: Rizzoli International Publications, 1990.
8 Hilberseimer, Ludwig, et al. *Metropolisarchitecture and Selected Essays*. New York: GSAPP Books, 2013.
9 Ibid., p. 24.
10 Ibid., p. 87.
11 Hilberseimer, Ludwig, et al. *Metropolisarchitecture and Selected Essays*. New York: GSAPP Books, 2013, pp. 120–121.
12 Ibid., p. 122.
13 Conrads, Ulrich, editor. *Programs and Manifestoes on 20th Century Architecture*. Cambridge, MA: MIT Press, 1971.
14 Wright, Frank Lloyd. *Broadacre City*. Tucson, AZ: University of Arizona Press, 1995.
15 Wright, Frank Lloyd. "Broadacre City. A New Community Plan." *Architectural Record*, vol. 77, Apr. 1935, pp. 243–254.
16 "Frank Lloyd Wright and the City: Density vs. Dispersal: Moma." *The Museum of Modern Art*, www.moma.org/calendar/exhibitions/1410.
17 Sert, Josep Lluis. "The Human Scale in City Planning." *New Architecture and City Planning: A Symposium*, edited by Paul Zucker. New York: Philosophical Library, 1971, pp. 392–412.
18 Sert, Josep Lluis. *Centres of Community Life*. Hoddesdon: CIAM 8 Conference, 1951.
19 Ibid., p. 6.

20 Den, Heuvel Dirk van, et al. *Alison and Peter Smithson: From the House of the Future to a House of Today*. Rotterdam: 010 Publishers, 2004, p. 62.
21 Ibid., p. 62.
22 Sbriglio, Jacques, et al. *L'unité D'habitation De Marseille: Le Corbusier*. Ed. Parenthèses, Taylor and Francis Online, 1992.
23 Cunha Borges, João, and Teresa Marat-Mendes. "Walking on Streets-in-the-Sky: Structures for Democratic Cities." *Journal of Aesthetics & Culture*, vol. 11, no. 1, 2019, pp. 1–15, https://doi.org/10.1080/20004214.2019.1596520.
24 Sbriglio, Jacques, et al. *L'unité D'habitation De Marseille: Le Corbusier*. Ed. Parenthèses, 1992, p. 3.
25 Sbriglio, Jacques. *Le Corbusier: L'unité D'habitation De Marseille Et Les Autres unités D'habitation à rezé-Les-Nantes, Berlin, Briey En forêt Et Firminy = unité D'habitation in Marseilles and the Four Other unité Blocks in rezé-Les-Nantes, Berlin, Briey En forêt and Firminy*. Basel: Fondation Le Corbusier, 2004.
26 Pedret, Annie. "Aix-En-Provence (France) 19–26 July 1953 CIAM IX: Discussing the Charter of Habitat." *Team 10*, www.team10online.org/team10/meetings/1953-Aix.htm.
27 Smithson, Alison Margaret, and Peter Smithson. *Ordinariness and Light: Urban Theories 1952–1960 and Their Application in a Building Project 1963–1970*. London: Faber and Faber, 1970, pp. 18–61.
28 Smithson, Peter. *The Charged Void: Urbanism*. London: The Monacelli Press, 2005, p. 26.
29 Smithson, Alison Margaret, and Peter Smithson. *The Charged Void: Architecture*. London: Monacelli Press, 2002, p. 84.
30 Frampton, Kenneth, and Alison Smithson. "Team 10 Primer." *Leonardo*, vol. 2, no. 2, 1969, p. 201, http://doi.org/10.2307/1572031.
31 Smithson, Alison Margaret, and Peter Smithson. *The Charged Void: Architecture*. London: Monacelli Press, 2002, p. 84.
32 Söderqvist, Lisbeth. "Structuralism in Architecture: A Definition." *Journal of Aesthetics & Culture*, vol. 3, no. 1, 2011, p. 5414, p. 2, http://doi.org/10.3402/jac.v3i0.5414.
33 Hertzberger, Herman. *Architecture and Structuralism: The Ordering of Space*. Edited by Els Brinkman. Translated by John Kirkpatrick. Rotterdam: Nai010 Publishers, 2015, p. 33.
34 Söderqvist, Lisbeth. "Structuralism in Architecture: A Definition." *Journal of Aesthetics & Culture*, vol. 3, no. 1, 2011, p. 5414, p. 2, http://doi.org/10.3402/jac.v3i0.5414.
35 Hertzberger, Herman. *Architecture and Structuralism: The Ordering of Space*. Edited by Els Brinkman. Translated by John Kirkpatrick. Rotterdam: Nai010 Publishers, 2015, p. 50.
36 Roberts, Rebecca, et al. *Moma Highlights: 375 Works from the Museum of Modern Art, New York*. New York: Museum of Modern Art, 2019.
37 Ibid.
38 Kinkela, David. "The Ecological Landscapes of Jane Jacobs and Rachel Carson." *American Quarterly*, vol. 61, no. 4, 2009, pp. 905–928, p. 917, https://doi.org/10.1353/aq.0.0115.

39 "Buildings & Projects." *Paul Rudolph Foundation*, https://paulrudolph.org/buildings-projects/.
40 Bruegmann, Robert, and Paul Rudolph. "Interview with Paul Rudolph / Interviewed by Robert Bruegmann, Compiled under the Auspices of the Chicago Architects Oral History Project, the Ernest R. Graham Study Center for Architectural Drawings, Department of Architecture, the Art Institute of Chicago." *Chicago Architects Oral History Project*, 1993, pp. 1–66, p. 34.
41 Friedman, Yona. *Yona Friedman: Pro Domo*. Barcelona: ACTAR, 2006, p. 65.
42 Ibid., pp. 65–69.
43 McDonough, Thomas F. "Situationist Space." *October*, vol. 67, 1994, pp. 58–77, p. 62.
44 Ibid., p. 59.
45 Ibid., p. 60.
46 McDonough, Thomas F. "Situationist Space." *October*, vol. 67, 1994, pp. 58–77, p. 64.
47 Wigley, Mark. *Constant's New Babylon: The Hyper-Architecture of Desire*. Rotterdam: 010 Publishers, 1998, p. 93.
48 Nieuwenhuys, Constant. "Constant's New Babylon on Permanent Display." *Kunstmuseum Den Haag*, 1 Oct. 2019, www.kunstmuseum.nl/en/constants-new-babylon-permanent-display.
49 McDonough, Tom. *The Activist Drawing: Retracing Situationist Architectures from Constant's New Babylon to Beyond*, edited by Zegher M. Catherine De and Mark Wigley. Cambridge, MA: MIT Press, 2001, p. 96.
50 Koolhaas, Rem, and Hans Ulrich Obrist. *Project Japan Metabolism Talks.* Cologne: Taschen GmbH, 2011, p. 106.
51 Originally appeared in: Kawazoe, Noboru, et al. *Metabolism: The Proposals for a New Urbanism*. Tokyo: Bijutsu Shuppansha, 1960.
   Republished: Koolhaas, Rem, and Hans Ulrich Obrist. *Project Japan Metabolism Talks.* Cologne: Taschen GmbH, 2011, p. 207.
52 Koolhaas, Rem, and Hans Ulrich Obrist. *Project Japan Metabolism Talks.* Cologne: Taschen GmbH, 2011, p. 336.
53 Maki, Fumihiko, and Masato Ohtaka. *Some Thoughts on Collective Form; with an Introduction to Group-Form*. St Louis: Washington University, 1961.
54 Ibid., p. 6.
55 Ibid., p. 14.
56 Essay taken from: Koolhaas, Rem, and Bruce Mau. *S, M, L, XL*. New York: Monacelli Press, 1998.
57 Ibid.
58 Susteren, Arjen van. *Metropolitan World Atlas*. Rotterdam: 010 Publishers, 2007.
59 Burdett, Ricky, and Deyan Sudjic. *The Endless City*. New York: Phaidon Press Limited, 2010.
60 Picon, Antoine. *Smart Cities: A Spatialised Intelligence*. Chichester: Wiley, 2015.

61 Allen, Stan. *Points + Lines: Diagrams and Projects for the City*. New York: Princeton Architectural Press, 2012.
62 Ibid., p. 52.
63 Waldheim, Charles. *The Landscape Urbanism Reader*. New York: Princeton Architectural Press, 2006.
64 Waldheim, Charles. *Landscape as Urbanism: A General Theory*. Princeton, NJ: Princeton University Press, 2016.
65 Frampton, Adam, et al. *Cities Without Ground: A Hong Kong Guidebook*. Novato, CA: ORO, 2018.
66 Weiss, Marion, and Michael A. Manfredi. *Public Natures: Evolutionary Infrastructures*. New York: Princeton Architectural Press, 2015.
67 Frampton, Kenneth. "The Generic Street as a Continuous Built Form." *On Streets*, edited by Stanford Anderson. Cambridge, MA: MIT Press, 1986, pp. 308–337.
68 Ibid., p. 309.
69 Ibid., p. 312.

3   Nine Typological Islands

The sprawling condition of megacities is a contemporary concern as the management of resources and planning for urban growth is increasingly more challenging. As previously stated, projected infra-architectural proposals from the 1960s focused on an architectural approach for controlling such urban expansion through megaform frameworks. These in turn would allow organic growth through plug-in units that would connect to the framework. The city of Seoul demonstrates such a structure as an infra-architecture model with an underground megastructure and urban blocks that work like architectural typological island formations. Architectural typological islands will refer to an urban condition where a specific typology is repeated as a "collective form"[1] and can be understood as an urban subunit. For Seoul, these typological islands have developed through tumultuous urban transformations due to drastic social, economical, and political shifts over the past 600 years. The Joseon Dynasty (1394–1897) followed an isolationist agenda, the Daehan Empire (1897–1910) opened to modernization, the Japanese Colonial rule (1910–1945) sought assimilation, the post-war era (1953–1988) promoted growth through industrialization, the globalization era (1988–2002) promoted Seoul to the world as a global city, and the cultural capital (2002–present) is testing the fourth industrial revolution and shared economies. Each transformation had to also endure variations in population starting with 100,000 people during the Joseon Dynasty,[2] 200,000 during the Daehan Empire,[3] 1 million at the top of the Japanese Colonial period,[4] 6 million during its industrialization period,[5] 8 million during its globalization period,[6] and topping at 10 million at the turn of the century.[7] Throughout all these periods Seoul maintained a highly planned framework through the evolutionary layering of its infrastructure, which resulted in compartmentalized architectural typological enclaves. This particular condition of Seoul offers an alternative method for analyzing urban mutations through its subunits of typological architectural islands, forming a reading of a megacity as an architectural project that defines a role of architecture in urbanism.

It is an uncontested reality that the world is inevitably becoming more urban. The abundant research that backs this claim by organization such as

DOI: 10.4324/9781032684963-3

the World Economic Forum,[8] along with the United Nations bi-annual World Urbanization Prospects report,[9] tends to point to the statement that a bit over half of the world population (UN reports 55%) live in urban areas.[10] This statement becomes critical when there is no clear demarcation of what really constitutes an "urban" condition as is the case for the European Commission claiming there is an 84% urban coverage instead by using different metrics.[11] Despite the different methodologies for reading urbanity, the incertitude for a consensus of reading urban areas raises the issue of identifying boundaries. An architectural typological island approach could provide a better account for an urban construct as it clearly demarcates bounded subunits, which can provide both quantitative and qualitative data.

One particular contemporary methodology from the NYU Urban Expansion Program led by Schlomo Angel defines urbanization as the project of moving people from the proximity of the land to a proximity to each other producing built settlements of different densities.[12] The settlements can be mapped as gradated 30 m pixelations in a 1 km grid that produce a heat map between urban (over 50% concentration), suburban (25–50% concentration), rural (under 25% concentration), and the fringe open spaces (remaining space). This methodology visualizes edge conditions for different urban levels, aiming at registering an *extrema tectorum* to produce "the city as a unit of analysis."[13] While this methodology can visualize the urban growth megacities have over time, more accurately measuring percentages of urbanity as defined by the researchers, it lacks a qualitative reading of the built environment that makes up that conurbation. These methods do not differentiate between high-rise and low-rise typologies, if it is a formally planned grid or an informal slum settlement. This presents a challenge for the organization and reading of megacities through an architectural lens, both from a quantitative planning perspective and an architectural qualitative state of its urban spaces.

As the project of urbanization is in a continuous process of expansion, which is polycentric in nature, it requires not the concept of the traditional city as a unit of analysis, but bounded subunits that allow for an organized flexible amalgamation. The reading of subunits and groupings allows for an additional layer of qualitative information to be displayed. Abercrombie's "potato" plan was one such methodology that focused on mapping the community structure of London through a "social and functional" analytical diagram of "social groupings and major use zones."[14] This became a comprehensive regional map of London and a way for understanding and planning its sprawl. "The plan poetically illustrates that an urban agglomeration consists of a large number of communities and centralities of distinct characters, which are both more or less self-sufficient and part of a larger organism at the same time."[15]

Although this methodology does represent the importance of urban subunits for understanding urbanity through an additional layer of information (in this case social constructs), it lacks the qualitative representation of the built environment. This might be better explored through architectural typological islands. This methodology is closely associated with the work led by Oswald Matthias Ungers for the redevelopment of a dispersed and fragmented post-war West Berlin as an archipelago of architectural islands. The notion of presenting the city as a set of urban islands introduces a new conception that counters an urbanization of an expansive infinite grid and focuses on the finality of bounded subunits. In 1977, Ungers, along with colleagues from Cornell, Rem Koolhaas, Pieter Riemann, Hans Kollhoff, and Arthur Ovaska, engaged on the project to define Berlin as a depopulated state composed of an archipelago of urban pockets framed as "cities within a city."[16] The project would become a manifesto and critique to traditional planning, presented in a series of Proposals by the Sommer Akademie for Berlin that would outline the project as a series of 11 thesis statements, comments, and conclusions.

This was an initial instance that urbanization had faced a reversal from expansion to contraction. In summary of the Proposals by the Sommer Akademie for Berlin, the team had identified that in the coming decade of the eighties, the population of Berlin would drop by another 10%.[17] This would contribute to further detriment as the anxiety would settle in the remaining population. Any solution to the problem would have to account for the improvement in quality of life to the remaining fabric while considering the reduction in density. These improvements cannot rely on the nostalgia of restoring a historical state that would never be achieved given the new density demands. Depopulation was to be treated as a global phenomenon, occurring in cities around the world as populations adopt a new lifestyle serviced by new technologies such as the car and the television that drives them out of the city centers, as well as other factors such as a loss of industry driving labor elsewhere. Cities like Brooklyn, NY, turned empty spaces into urban farming, optimizing the depopulation while safeguarding the key parts of the city. Depopulated cities could then be conceptualized as archipelagos with key parts of the city completed as enclaves after their selection and justification for their preservation. These enclaves could be completed by assimilating typologies from other places that can be transplanted in the desired islands in order to generate a desired characteristic. The green space between islands would be used for low-density housing, temporary housing and spaces for production and leisure.

For Koolhaas, the idea of the island had already been synthesized through the "City of Captive Globe (1972),"[18] which dealt with urbanization as the possible scenario for impossibilities to occur through the regularization of infrastructure as architecture. A solid podium gets repeated in a grid, conceptually an equalizing capitalist block that unifies the urban logic. The podium, which demarcates the grid, allows for endless possible configurations of skyscrapers to exist on top. In the "City of Captive Globe," Koolhaas populates each podium block with a different iconic building that portrays the possible heterogeneity that can occur within the homogeneous grid. This would signify each block as its own island, its own "city within a city" at the scale of a building rather than Ungers's enclaves. The buildings identified within the "City of Captive Globe" represent a range of manifestos that are allowed for all to exist in the same infrastructural plane, such as an abstraction of Ungers's Architecture, Religion in ruins, two towers of Le Corbusier's Plan Voisin, Das Cabinet des Dr. Caligari, the Waldorf-Astoria Hotel, an homage to Mies van der Rohe, Dali's Ángelus arquitectónico de Millet, Ivan Leonidov's Ministry of Heavy Industry, El Lissitsky's Lenin's stand, Malevitch's Architekton, The RCA Building in New York City, Rockefeller Center, an homage to Super-studio, Trylon, and Perisphere by Wallace Harrison, and an abstraction of the Berlin Wall.

Ungers's idea of the island also captivated Colin Rowe who, along with Fred Koetter, introduced the notion of the "Collage City"[19] in 1978. Rowe's notion of the island dealt more with topological orders that form the urban space based on historical typologies. Rowe's analysis of architectural prec-edents that formed successful public spaces like plazas, could be abstracted by their massing and transplanted to produce new spaces. The collage city would then be formed by islands of these topologies of urban spaces represented by their figure-ground, which is arguably the wrong interpretation of what Ungers intended with his islands. For Seoul, the term "island" is more closely aligned with O. M. Ungers and the idea of a "city within a city," autonomous enclaves of recognizable typologies.

In the contemporary state of Seoul, nine architectural island typologies can be distinctly identified to work as autonomous urban blocks. These have been categorized through field observation, historical mappings, zoning regu-lations, and real estate classifications of typologies. Seoul's nine typological blocks are the political form block, the iconic form block, apartment block, megaform block, superblock, tower block, deep block, podium block, and the cultural block. Each block represents a bounded condition that serves as an autonomous architectural unit of urbanity, repeated throughout the city. Each block typology can be studied independently through its quantitative and qualitative properties via case studies that present the possibility of read-ing Seoul as a megacity – a product of architecture, not an endless sprawl, and a product of urbanism. The following is an explanation for each of the nine blocks that will serve as urban subunits. In order to give a contextual back-ground, the architectural typological islands are explained through a historical recount of six periods where specific regimes guided the urban development of Seoul; each period producing particular typological islands.

Joseon Dynasty Period (1394–1896)

In 1392, Yi Seong-gye, King Taejo posthumously, founded the Joseon Dy-nasty.[20] Following his ascension to the throne, King Taejo decides to relo-cate the capital of the new dynasty to a more central location accessible to all the people of the kingdom. From records of the Annals of King Taejo,[21] it is recorded that on the eleventh day of August, 1394, King Taejo himself inspected the foothills of Muak Mountain and Baekaksan Mountain. After consulting with Buddhist Master Muhak and through recommendations of the Privy Council, King Taejo decides on the new site where Seoul sits today. This was to become Hanyang, the new capital of the Joseon Dynasty.[22]

> The king was elated and said, "Now looking at this topography, it can be used for the royal capital. What's more, (the river) can be navigated by transport ships and it is centrally located (the distance here is about the same distance from all directions within the kingdom), providing convenience to the people."[23]

Seoul was founded in 1394 under the principles of geomancy and Confucian philosophy, which also carried city form guidelines.[24] Through these principles, Seoul was laid out in a valley surrounded by four mountains (Bugaksan in the North, Inwangsan in the West, Namsan in the South, and Naksam in the East) that would filter the right amount of energy, chi.[25] The streams and tributaries forming in the mountains would merge in a central stream, Cheonggyecheon, which served as the water supply for the city. Gyeongbokgung palace, built in 1395,[26] sat at the foot of the Northern mountain. The Royal Family Ancestral Shrine also built in 1395, Jognmyo Shrine, would sit to the East, and Sajikdan Altar to the deities of soil and grains built in 1395 would sit to the West.[27] An 18.6-km long fortress wall would enclose the entire city in 1396,[28] connecting all four mountains and allowing entry into the city through eight gates: Bukdaemun/Sukjeongmun (North gate, built in 1396),[29] Dongsomun/Hyehwamun (Northeast gate, built in 1396),[30] Dongdaemun/Heunginjimun (East gate, built in 1396),[31] Namsomun/Gwanghuimun (Southeast gate, built in 1396),[32] Namdaemun/Sungnyemun (South gate, built in 1396),[33] Seosomun/Souimun (Southwest gate, built in 1396),[34] Seodaemun/Donuimun (West gate, built in 1396),[35] and Buksomun/Changuimun (Northwest gate, built in 1396).[36] Its four main gates would correspond to the Confucian elements, East for wood, West for gold, South for fire, North for water, and earth was represented by the Bosingak Belfry in the middle of the city as explained by Todd Henry.[37] The Royal Confucian Academy (currently Sungkyunkwan University) was built in 1398[38] in the Northeast of the city establishing the first institution. The Six Ministries street was also developed creating the main axis of the city (north-south) starting at Gyeongbokgung palace.[39]

The layering of geomantic principles and the Confucian philosophy in Hanyang's original composition planned by King Taejo, organized the city as a ritualistic political construct defined by its architectural elements. First, there is an overall bounding city form marked by the fortress wall with its eight gates, which served as a military infrastructure. Similar to ancient cities and fortress European cities, the delimitation of city growth within the walls served an administrative purpose of control over the subjects.[40] Second, the

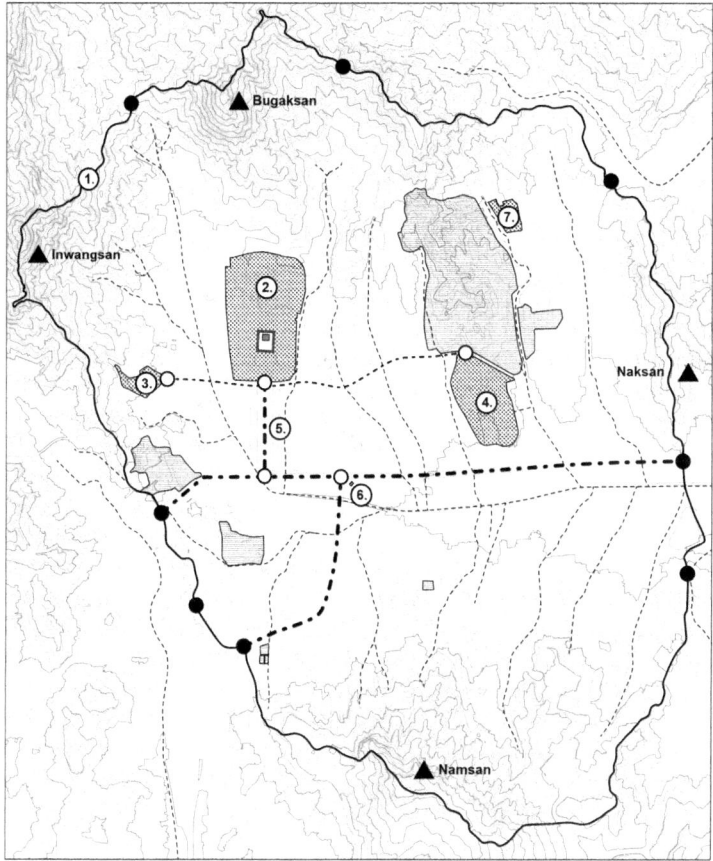

1. Fortress Wall
2. Gyeongbokgung
3. Sajikdan
4. Jongmyo Shrine
5. Six Ministries Street
6. Bosingak Belfry
7. Royal Confucian Academy

Figure 3.1 Original composition of Seoul during the Joseon Dynasty.

palace complex of the king served as the civic core where the ruler and central government would occupy the city. Third, the Sajikdan Altars to the west and Jongmyo shrine to the east of the palace formed an east-west axis as the king would exit the palace and travel between these two. "Jongmyo and Sajikdan were symbols of dynamic legitimacy and therefore the first structures erected when a new state is founded."[41] Fourth, a north-south axis would be flanked by the construction of the Six Ministries Street, Yukjogeori. This was the boulevard that would lead to the palace's main gate. The buildings on the east side of the street consisted of the State Council, Ministry Personnel, Hanseongbu (Capital Prefecture or a modern-day City Hall), Ministry of Taxation, and Bureau of Elder Statesmen. On the west side resided the Ministry of Rites, Office of Inspector General, Ministry of War, Ministry of Punishment, and Ministry of Public Works.[42] The street would represent the space of interaction where government officials would work, the King's decrees would be heard, and the general subjects would voice their concerns. Fifth, The Royal Confucian Academy was established the same year for the purpose of training candidates for the lower Civil Service Examinations. Perceived as the highest institution for learning in the kingdom, it could instruct 200 candidates.[43] The system for training government officials was later expanded with four additional government schools, Central, Western, Southern, and Eastern schools. Lastly, the Cheonggyecheon worked as a water infrastructure running West to East due to the geography of the valley. Unjongga, current day Jong-ro, became the main street in the city for people to gather as a public space, running parallel to the Cheonggyecheon. The Bosingak Belfry would represent the symbolic center,[44] sitting right on Unjongga and to the east of where Yukjogeori would end perpendicularly at Unjongga. A second north-south street would form from Namdaemun gate to the Bosingak Belfry as Unjongga became the commercial center once King Taejong had government licensed stores built along Unjongga in order to supply the palace with goods.[45] Namdaemun gate represented the main connection to the rest of the Kingdom, and this is where people would bring their goods to sell. Merchants would sell around the Southern gate, and connect to Unjongga as the commercial center.

Regardless of the concentration of power within the confinements of the fortress walls and palaces, the jurisdiction of the capital included an area also outside the walls that expanded to about 4 km from the walls (10 *Li*), also referred to as Seongjeosimni.[46] The regional capital of Joseon, Hanseongbu, included districts outside the walls like Mapo, and Yongsan for commerce and districts like Wangsimni and Seogang for agriculture. These areas outside the walls became largely populated during the late Joseon period comprising about half of the total residents of the capital city. Government offices were also necessary outside the walls as well as additional symbolic spaces like altars and shrines. Warehouses outside the walls stored military provisions, grains, and ice.

Ten main roads were built to connect the capital to the rest of the empire, six of them by the mid-18th century, three more by the end of the 18th century, and the last road, by the end of the 19th century.[47] These main roads provided government posts and lodging facilities to supply traveling officials with meals, lodging, and horses. Although anyone in the kingdom could use the roads, they also represented the extent of the power emitted from the central core, the capital city.

Political Form Block

Based on the *Rites of Zhou*, the original form of the capital should have been a square, but due to the geographical conditions the fortress took more of an ellipse form.[48] The elliptical fortress, a military infrastructure, is the recognizable structure that defines a clear administrative control and a demarcation for what is inside the city versus outside. This bounded separation, common for fortress cities around the world, also occurred at an architectural level within Seoul through the composition of the royal grounds that became the political form block typology. The political form parallels "Absolute Architecture," theorized by Pier Vitori Aureli.[49] Aureli defines the condition of "absolute" as one that cuts itself from the rest in order to have an autonomous formal separation. In the case of Seoul, the political form physically encloses itself from the rest of the city, controlling its own ground and asserting its domain. At a regional scale, the fortress wall produces this effect, defining that which is city and that which is nature, while at an architectural

Figure 3.2 Gyeongbokgung as the original *political form block*.

scale, the royal grounds orchestrated the center of power within the city. With the ascension of new kings, the center of power would shift gradually and would take an active role in the ritualistic organization of the city within the fortress wall. The centers of authority in Seoul would relocate as new palace complexes were built. King Taejong, who ascended to the throne in 1400, had a second palace, Changdeokgung, built in 1405.[50] Under King Sejong, Changgyeonggung was built for his father, King Taejong, in the mid-1400s.[51] In 1483, King Seongjong renovated and enlarged Changgyeonggung.[52] During the Imjin War (1592–1598), palaces as well as altars and shrines suffered from the Japanese first invasion.[53] Palace halls and government offices were destroyed by fire. The destruction of Gyeongbokgung, Changdeokgung, and Changgyeonggung limited King Seonjo to take over a collection of residential buildings that belonged to the royal ancestral family as the temporary palace named Deoksugung as the rebuilding process begins after the war.[54] Gyeongbokgung is left destroyed, Changdeokgung is rebuilt in 1609, Changgyeonggung is rebuilt in 1616, and a new palace, Gyeonghuigung, is completed in 1623.[55] Deoksugung becomes the auxiliary palace as Changdeokgung becomes the primary palace housing the royal court and seat of government from 1609 until Gyeongbokgung is rebuilt in 1867 and retakes the position of primary palace in 1868.[56]

Despite the relocation or addition of palaces, shrines, altars, and other royal institutions, these buildings have been archived as essential components with the same formal representation of an enclosed typology throughout the mappings of the Joseon Dynasty. Starting with the Comprehensive Map of the Eight Provinces of Joseon (1685),[57] Map of the Capital (1770s),[58] Map of Seoul (1830),[59] Map of the Capital (1853–1856),[60] Map of the Capital (1861),[61] and Map of the Capital (Atlas of Joseon 19th century),[62] the city is only represented through the fortress wall, royal grounds, and geographical context with no indication of an urban fabric. Palaces are walled, as well as the Royal Confucian Academy, Jongmyo Shrine, Sajikdan Altar, a Temple for the King's Portraits to the South, and royal grounds adjacent to Changgyeonggung and Deoksugung.

Confined by a defensive wall, each royal ground (palace, or shrine) would separate itself from the rest of the generic city fabric as autonomous forms that disregard transformations that occur around them. The royal grounds of Seoul, in that sense, represent the collective memory of the city, producing a diagram of the city that maintains a contextual permanence despite any changes to the city fabric around them.

This separation from the rest of the city was also manifested in the modular growth that occurred inside the royal grounds, unlike the generic urban fabric outside the royal grounds. In an almost Structuralist logic, an additive module formed rooms that would be added as needed, depending on the size of the complex. The module was used for the production of covered arcades, halls, and residential rooms as a continuous architectural network.

To further understand the political form block as an island, it is necessary to contextualize within its surrounding urban fabric. During the Joseon Dynasty a single-family, single-use building infilled the space in-between streams, and between the royal grounds.[63] The natural tributaries would form the template for the basic neighborhood boundaries and a network of streets.[64] Cheonggyecheon along with Unjongga would have the effect of sectioning the city between North and South of the stream, and the middle area between Unjongga and Cheonggyecheon. Bukchon was classified as the village to the North of this axis, housing nobility due to the proximity to Gyeongbokgung to the west, and later Changdeokgung to the east.[65] Namchon, the village to the South of Cheonggyecheon became occupied by Confucian Academics, while technical specialists resided in the center, Jungchon.[66] Despite the classification of neighborhoods by social strata, the typology used for the generic fabric was the same single-family, single-use "hanok," Korean style house.

Mostly facing a southern orientation, hanoks would form courtyards and infill the spaces between streams with separations of 1 m between buildings achieving a low-rise high-density fabric. Based on the remaining hanok fabrics found in Seoul today (Bukchon used for this example), hanok achieved a 60% building coverage ratio, but a floor area ratio of 0.60 since the hanok typology is a single-story building.[67] Based on data from the Center for International Affairs in Korea and The Academy of Korean Studies, a census from 1428 shows 16,921 households inside the city walls and only 1,601 outside the walls, with a population of 103,328 inside the city and 6,044 outside the city.[68] By 1789 there were 22,094 households inside the city and 21,835 outside the city with a population of 112,371 inside and 76,782 outside.[69] What this data shows is that a higher pressure on the housing needs was put outside the walls as the population increased but the typology could not support the density.

Daehan Empire Period (1897–1910)

Singular Iconic Form Block

Gojong ascended to the throne in 1863 at the age of 12, but due to his age his father was granted the title of Daewongun in order to rule under Gojong's name until he reached adulthood.[70] The Daewongun aimed to protect the kingdom from any foreign ideas by enforcing an isolationist policy, which eventually led to protective battles against the French squadron in 1866 and the U.S. Asiatic Squadron in 1871.[71] In 1874, when King Gojong came of age, the Daewongun had to retire from his power.[72] This transfer of power along with the invasions by French and American forces was seen by the Japanese as a new opportunity to open the ports of Korea in Japan's favor. With a show of force, the Japanese navy coerced Korea to sign the Treaty of Ganghwa (Japan–Korea Treaty of 1876).[73] The treaty ended the tributary state status of the Joseon Dynasty to the Qing Dynasty in China and allowed Japan to open three ports – Busan, Incheon, and Wonsan – while granting extraterritoriality to Japanese living in Korea.[74]

During this time, Queen Min took an important role in politics and directed much of Joseon's policies. In 1877, Queen Min and King Gojong, ordered a mission to Japan in order to investigate the westernization process and the intentions from Japan toward Korea.[75] In 1881, a second mission was conducted in Japan in order to report on the status of Tokyo and Osaka, which was westernized throughout the Meiji Restoration and now overpowered Seoul as new Asian centers.[76] During this second mission, Kim Hongjip, then a diplomat of Korea, met with the Chinese ambassador to Tokyo, Ho Ju-chang and the councilor Huang Tsun-hsien, who presented Kim with a book written by Huang called the "Korean Strategy."[77] China was threatened by Russian encroachment into east Asia and saw Korea as a barrier from Japanese expansion into the mainland as well. With a looming threat from Japan toward China and Korea, Queen Min was advised to take a pro-Chinese police force, maintain the status quo with Japan and create new alliances with the West, specifically with the United States.[78]

During the next two decades, foreign relations treaties were signed between Korea and the United States, Germany, United Kingdom, Russia, and France among others.[79] Foreign legations opened in Jeong-dong, establishing the neighborhood as the new focal center of Seoul and introducing a new architectural typology, the iconic form typology through the foreign legation buildings. These were Western Style buildings that separated themselves as free standing autonomous landmarks, uninhibited by any dense urban fabric in order to showcase the presence of an international affiliation. The legations would transform the landscape in Jeong-dong with the construction of these western style buildings opening their own churches, hospitals, schools, and hotels, creating a tripartite city between Western, Chinese, and Japanese settlements. This new restructuring of the city through neighborhoods breaks the original symbolic and ritualistic organization from Joseon and establishes a new center in the city not characteristic of the royal ground political form, but by a field of iconic buildings, the grouping of which would constitute a singular island composition.

After the first Sino-Japanese War of 1894, Japan obtained control over Korea installing a new government and declaring Korea independent from China allowing Japan to instate the Gabo Reforms, similar to the Meiji Restoration.[80] This reform sought to end the feudal economic and social system, modernizing the country. This has an urban effect of organizing the main axis through the demolition of makeshift commercial structures in Namdaemun and along Jongno. New buildings along these streets have to follow newly enacted guidelines as regulations on the widths of the streets were also announced by 1896.[81]

Politically, an anti-Japanese sentiment began to grow in the early 1890s. The Queen Consort is seen as a threat by the Japanese and a plot is formed to remove her from power.[82] In 1895, the brutal assassination of the queen took place through the occupation of her residence in Gyeongbokgung. King Gojong escapes this attack and is protected by seeking refuge at the Russian legation along with the prince in 1896. The King ruled from this location for almost a year until through the pressure of foreign powers and the newly formed Independence Club of 1896, King Gojong returned to Gyeongung-gung to re-establish his presence of power.[83]

Gyeongunggung served as a collection of royal residences and was adapted in 1896 to become an official palace when King Gojong returned in 1897. Upon his return, Gojong declares the formation of the Daehan Empire and is crowned as the first emperor declaring the independence of Korea and the beginning of a new era through the Gwangmu Reforms.[84] These reforms would continue the push for modernization of the capital through the implementation of Western technologies throughout the following 10 years.

Gyeongunggung is built to establish a new center of power surrounded by the foreign legations, and a new road connects back to the Six Ministries street.[85] Junghwajeon Hall (Throne Hall) is built along with Hwangudan (Altar to Heaven) establishing a new composition for the center of Seoul as an area consisting of a mixture of western buildings and palace structures rather than a clear political form.[86] Influenced by the iconic form typologies, the palace itself was expanded with Jeonggwanheon in 1900 by A. I. Sabatin, a Russian architect.[87]

This new center composition was further enhanced with the establishment of the Hanseong Electric Company in 1898,[88] which allowed for the electrification of the palace along with the establishment of a new infrastructural right of way for the first streetcar line in Jongno.[89] The streetcar naturally followed the path of the electric cables forming new infrastructural bundling along main streets and demarcating the Jeong-dong district as an enclave of western buildings. King Gojong was forced out of the throne and Sunjong, his son, ascended to the throne in 1907.[90] By this time, Seoul had been transformed from a city organized by a Confucian diagram of rituals to one of modern infrastructure and iconic forms.

Japanese Occupation Period (1910–1945)

Dispersed Iconic Form Block

Following the 1904 Russo Japanese War, Korea had fallen under the protectorate of Japan through the imposition of the Japan–Korea Treaty of 1905.[91] This was opposed by Emperor Gojong who sought international aid to delegitimize the treaty by sending an envoy to the Hague Conference of World Peace. This effort yielded no positive results, ending in Gojong's forceful stepping down on July 18 of 1907, and replaced by his son, Sunjong, by Japanese appointment enforcing the Japan–Korea Treaty of 1907.[92] In 1910,

Figure 3.3 The urban void from the Old City Hall has become a contemporary plaza.

the Japanese Minister of War carried out the mission to complete the takeover of Korea, finalizing its annexation to Japan with the Japan–Korea Treaty of 1910.[93] Already deprived of foreign and internal affairs by the two previous treaties, Japan takes governing control of Korea by setting Keijo/ Gyeongseong (Seoul) as the colonial capital with Terauchi Masatake appointed as the first Governor-General of Korea. Japan would continue the modernization process that had begun with the Gwangmu reforms and would use the Meiji Restorations done in Tokyo and Osaka as a model for the colonial capital. This resulted in the implementation of land reform policies and the restructuring of the capital for the purpose to assimilate the colony as part of the Japanese Empire.

For the first 15 years, spatial interventions in the capital focused on disarranging the Joseon symbolic structure with the purpose of establishing the subordination of the colony and disrupting the collective memory of Hanseong.[94] This disruption in the city makeup was operated through three spatial strategies: the reconfiguration of the political form typology, reintroduction of the iconic form typology for slum clearing and redevelopment, and establishment of an expansion project of urbanization through the use of a grid system. The first two strategies dealt with the destruction of the political form block and implementing a new iconic form block. The third strategy would mark a shift from city form to urbanization in Seoul.

The political form typologies, which were established through the privatization and control of a bounded ground, are reconfigured as open public grounds. Gyeonggungung was renamed Deoksugung in 1907 after the Japan–Korea Treaty of 1907.⁹⁵ Sunjong is relocated out of Deoksugung into Changdeokgung in order to disassociate this palace as the center of power. Seokjojeon Hall, a Neoclassical style art museum, was built in 1910 by British architect G. R. Harding as the palace is opened to the public.⁹⁶ Following the model of Ueno park in Tokyo, Changggyeonggung was transformed as a public park and zoo between 1908 and 1911.⁹⁷ Gyeonghuigung is stripped of its buildings as they are destroyed or sold, and the grounds turned into a school for Japanese citizens.⁹⁸ Lastly, and perhaps the most disruptive break from the political form was the restructuring of Gyeongbokgung as exhibition grounds and the site for the new Government General Building.⁹⁹ In preparation of the Government General Building, the inner structures of Gyeongbokgung were demolished, leaving only 10 out of the 400 original structures.¹⁰⁰ This tabula rasa became the site for the 1915 exhibition used to propagate the new order of modernization under Japanese control.

A main purpose of the exposition is to show people the current conditions of Korea during colonial rule: industrial progress, development of education, hygiene, civil engineering and finance. Yet, the exposition should avoid luxury installations and decorations in displays, maintaining simple and unadorned styles, in order to prompt further progress of industry and culture by showing an exact picture of the actual Korea. The detailed instructions will be added later, but I want you [the provincial governors] to fully understand the purpose and to make a greater effort to prepare a number of exhibits enough to show the real situation of industry and commerce in each province.¹⁰¹

Its aim was to replace the palace from a historical emblem of Joseon to an emblem of modernity.

The iconic form typology was reintroduced as a singular block typology that manifested the Japanese control as opposed to the open policy to foreign relations and trade that they symbolized during the Daehan Empire. These buildings represented symbolic landmarks for the new order. While they were still identified as having a western style architecture to represent modernization, they also served to replace any Joseon architectural icons. For example, the Keijo Kangoku (Keijo Prison) was built in 1908 to imprison

Korean activists seeking liberation.[102] The prison is placed on the grounds of the Independence Gate, which was originally built to inspire independence after the Sino-Japanese war. The Ring Hall Altar (Hwangudan) built in 1897 serves as another example. Built to commemorate the ascension of Gojon as Emperor, the structure was replaced by the Chosun Gyeongseong Railroad Hotel in 1913.[103] The Bank of Korea, designed by Tatsuno Kingo in 1907 and built in 1912[104] replaced any previous Joseon financial system with the new central bank in charge of printing Korean Yens. This building was grouped to form a public square with the Keijo Central Post Office Building (1913–1915) and later with the Mitsukoshi department store (1930) to serve the wealthier Japanese residents and establish the Japanese neighborhood as the highlight for the capital.[105] Deoksugung palace was also suppressed in importance as it progressively became surrounded with icons of new authority with buildings like a new City Hall (1925) across on the east of Deoksugung palace, the Gyeongseong Public Hall (Bumingwan Theater-1934), and the Government General's Communication Bureau's Business Center (1938) to the North, and the Keijo Judicial Building (1926–1928) to its South.

The most disruptive incision was the construction of the Government General Building in the grounds of Gyeongbokgung palace. This imposition on the most symbolic representational space of the Joseon Dynasty required its demolition with no means of preservation. Beginning construction in 1916, the building would occupy the space of Gwanghwamun gate and block any views toward Gyeongbokgung. Completed in 1926, the Government General Building would become the largest government building in East Asia at the time, which showed the importance that Keijo (Gyeongseong) had not only as a colonial capital, but as an example of the exuberance of the whole empire.[106]

Aside from displacing symbols of Joseon and Daehan Empire, these typologies would be used for urban reform as land clearing projects that eliminated blocks considered as slums. This process would form a new block typology where the iconic form would produce a boundary through a voided space. Based on the maps of 1927 and 1933, iconic building blocks represented about 25% of the total urban central area.[107] Unlike the political form that would create islands through solid physical boundary formations, the Iconic form would have the effect of generating islands through urban voids that would distance the building from the rest of the fabric as autonomous objects.

The third spatial strategy reconfigured Seoul from the confined city project to an expansive urbanization project where roads and neighborhoods reinforce capital accumulation as well as colonial control. To accommodate the imminent population growth, the capital needed to be modernized through an urbanization process, which meant breaking the city fortress model for an urbanization model,[108] borrowing from the German *Regulierung der städte* to promote sanitation, widening, and straightening the system of roads.[109] The expansion of Keijo required the demolition of the symbolic boundary formed by the fortress wall to be replaced by an administrative boundary based on the new mapped surveys. The wall was systematically demolished to allow for infrastructural expansion to the South connecting to the increasing settlements in Yongsan and its military posts. Yongsan would be further connected to the commercial area of Mapo to the West in the 1920s.[110] Parts of the wall were demolished in Seodaemun, Namdaemun, and Dongdaemun. The part of the wall near Namdaemun was replaced by a Shinto shrine in Namsan to replace a Joseon symbol for a Japanese public space.[111]

The urbanization of Keijo was carried out in two stages, the first from 1910 to 1919, and the second from 1919 to 1924.[112] During the first stage, Mochiji Rokusaburo (Head of the Civil Engineering Bureau) recommended following the model of Dalian, which had been based on a system of rotaries by Russian planners before 1905.[113] The Radial City proposed a series of diagonal streets to form plazas that would mark urban nodes (based on John Evelyn's Plan for Rebuilding the City of London 1666), which could be utilized to highlight new centers of power. Represented on the New Detailed Map of 1914, the intersection between Taihei Blvd and Jongno was meant to form the first plaza, which aimed to deter the attention from Deoksugung. A series of 42 gridded roads were planned to facilitate the real estate process for land ownership and more importantly its taxation. The Land Confiscation Law of 1911 enabled the process of recreating Japanese urban administrative units such as the Cho, Chome, and Machi.[114]

During the second phase, Taihei Blvd would be expanded to emphasize the new growth of the city in a north-south axis with the Government General Building as the focal endpoint at the North. Already in 1917 a new bridge over the Han river had been constructed to connect Yongsan to the South, which facilitated the north-south axis. Taihei Blvd was expanded to a width of 62 m and the new Keijo Train Station marked a new Southern node outside of Namdaemun.

By 1925, the population had increased to 342,000 from the previous 200,000 at the beginning of the colonization, and would reach 444,000 by 1935.[115] While the urbanization plans looked to parcelize most of the city, only 15 out of the 42 roads would be completed in the inner city. After the plan of 1928, the expansion of the administrative boundary would increase by 3.5× enacted in the Town Planning Act of 1936.[116] The population would eventually surpass 900,000 by 1940.[117] The population increase was in direct correlation to the urban expansion which would form the base for the modern metropolis.

This is a crucial point in the urban history of Seoul, as for the first time since the formation of Joseon, the mapping representation of the city was no longer based on architecture but on the infrastructural systems represented in the 1936 City District Planning Map, 1938 Rigid Urban Planning Map, The Metropolitan Road Map Planning Plan, and the Transportation Panning Map. Infrastructure expansion dominated city planning, while architecture served as infill. The Hanok was mass produced with additional rooms in order to maximize density.[118] Since this was primordial housing typology, it would still not form islands as they were meant to densify the generic urban fabric along with other newly implemented housing typologies imported by the Japanese.

Park Chung Hee Period (1963–1979)

Apartment Block

The independence of Korea, after the Japanese surrendered in 1945, was quickly followed by the Korean War from 1950 to 1953, which left Seoul in an impoverished and devastated state. After the armistice of 1953, the immigration from rural to urban rapidly surged, creating unplanned squatter settlements. The population grew from 1,569,000 in 1955 to 2,445,000 in 1960, increasing the density from 53 to 96 persons per hectare.[119] Jongno-gu, Jung-gu, and Dongdaemun-gu suffered the highest density pressure with

Figure 3.4 Apartment blocks in Gangnam.

squatters occupying public spaces. The street ratio of 8% in urban areas by 1961 also limited hygiene as congestion, pollution, and informal settlements exacerbated the already debilitated urban framework.[120] Shanty towns along the Cheonggyecheon, Ichon, and Majang materialized with the use of debris and found materials that would serve as shelters. The city government had a crippled budget that was inhibiting a proper development of urban districts at the time. The social and economic instability facilitated a military seizure of power in 1961 led by Kim Jong-pil.[121] Major General Park Chung Hee would emerge as the new leader of the country out of this military coup. Park Chung Hee had been a junior officer under the Japanese army and would withhold the Japanese doctrines for a strong nationalism, as well as a centralized control of the economy.[122] While the military controlled the political agencies, supervised by the newly formed Korean Central Intelligence Agency (KCIA) led by Kim Jong-pil, Park created the Economic Planning Board (EPB) in 1961.[123] By Park's mandate, the Economic Planning Board would be led by civilian experts with high technical qualifications for the aim to elevate Korea's economic policies. It would be the Economic Planning Board that would introduce the first in a series of five "Five Year Economic plans" that would not only reshape the economy for an export-oriented industrialization but also influence the spatial development with an almost authoritarian control as pointed out by Kim and Choe,

> the dominant political ideologies of government that drove the national priorities and agenda dictated how and what type of urban development should take place through various government programs and incentives. They ultimately shaped the outcome of urban spatial structures, without providing a forum for any meaningful discussion and participation from the general population.[124]

With the 1960s policies of heavy industrialization, immigration into urban centers flourished. The need to solve the pressing urban issues sparked the foundation of a new Urban Planning Bureau in 1961, and the Korea National Housing Corporation on July 1st of 1962 with the aim of providing housing for the lower income growing population.[125] In 1963, Seoul was yet again expanded in size, radically to 613 km^2, more than doubling its previous colonial boundary.[126] For Seoul, the need for an urban planning strategy along with mass housing quickly became primary agendas. This resulted in a series of visionary masterplans and the development of the apartment block typology.

The rigorous master planning of Seoul began with the first 10 year plan of 1965, which would become the Seoul Metro Area Plan of 1966, aimed at concentrating its development in focused areas within a limit of a 15 km radius from the historic fortress center in order to remain compact.[127] A greenbelt was also proposed at around the same radius that would encapsulate a primary street network of 13 radial streets and 4 circular ones. Six subcenters would be equally distributed around the old center in order to decentralize a projected population of over 5.5 million people within 20 years. By 1970, the population had already reached 5,536,000,[128] and it needed a more detailed plan for population and subcenters distribution fomented in the Revised Plan of 1970, which added one extra subcenter.

The Land Readjustment program, which had already begun under colonial rule, was also revamped during this masterplanning era in order to achieve a spatial order by securing land for public use and infrastructure. As defined by the city of Seoul:

> The Land Readjustment Program is a replotting-based approach, exchanging and subdividing/combining the land without altering the relationship of rights in existence prior to the program. This method of securing land for public facilities and developing built-up areas in the city was adopted as a way to prevent disorderly urban sprawl as the city grew in areas without sufficient financing. It also sought to acquire public land in new built-up areas in advance. One of the advantages of the program is that public land can be acquired without investing public resources as the land owner is compensated through replotting as per a certain percentage of lots on the land set out for public use or for other plans. Priority to become the program entity (and implement the program) is given to the land owner and the association. If this does not occur, the national government, local governments, the Korea Housing Corporation, or the Korea Land Development Corporation can implement it.[129]

One hundred and forty square kilometers were developed within 58 districts by means of land readjustment, representing about 40% of the total developable land in Seoul.[130] The main implication of this process is that of the urban housing island effect. Through the land readjustment program, smaller parcels could be combined into a single parcel in order to allow large constructions of apartment developments by a single entity backed by the Urban Planning Act and the Land Expropriation Act of 1962.[131] The Korea Housing corporation implemented the pilot project through the construction of the Mapo Apartment Complex in 1962 and the Civil Servant Apartment in 1966 in Ichon-dong.[132] The Mapo Apartment Complex would distribute 642 households among 10 buildings in a single unified parcel. This would produce a parcelization effect that would categorize a specific housing typology for such parcels. This allows for the parcel configuration to remain unchanged while the apartments get replaced for denser units while maintaining the typology over time.

The mismatch between the growing urban population and housing supply fomented the continued application of the land readjustment program with similar apartment constructions led by the Korean Housing Corporation. In 1965, the KNHC established over 132 million m² for future development in

Hwagok-dong, and during the 1970s it constructed 7,906 units in the Banpo Apartment Complex and 19,180 units in Jamsil.[133] From 1970 to 1989, the apartment type would increase from 4.1% of the total housing to 35.1% respectively.[134] While the detached dwelling would fall from a domineering 88.4% in 1970 to 46.1% by 1989. This signified a massive increase in the number of single parcel developments that would create urban islands through the designation of apartment complexes development areas in 1976 through the Urban Planning Act.[135] The act would designate land readjustment areas for development in Banpo, Apgujeong, Seocho, Dogok, Cheongdam, and Gaepo supplying 497,000 units within Seoul alone.[136]

Megaform Block

At the same time that the apartment parcels were being developed South of the Han River, a need to reinvigorate the central core grew among the planning

Figure 3.5 Megaforms in parallel to the Cheonggyecheon.

agendas. The city center had grown during the 1950s and 1960s as an urban slum filled with illegal housing by an impoverished immigrant population. Despite the efforts during the colonial period to redevelop the city center by planning newer infrastructure, much of the blocks stayed the same with narrow undulated pathways and single-story structures. After the implementation of the first Five Year Economic Plan, the city of Seoul revamped the efforts to modernize the city center that consisted of hundreds of small parcels making it difficult to produce unified larger projects. The Enforcement Decree of the Urban Planning Act was revised in 1965 introducing the mapping for redevelopment districts.[137] The designation of these districts didn't enforce any new parcelization, which limited the redevelopment at the time to land owned by the city. One of these consisted of a strip of land that originated from the Japanese colonial planning and their revision of the Air Defense Act from 1937 against fires from attacks. In order to protect the infrastructure in the city center, the act allowed the forceful removal of structures in order to prevent fire from spreading in the case of an attack. In 1943 a strip of land 50 m wide and 1,180 in length stretching from Jongmyo to Pildong was reserved as a fire breaker.[138] After the Korean War, the area was left unadministered resulting in illegal occupation by refugees and North Korean fugitives becoming an urban slum notorious for prostitution.[139] Mayor Kim Hyon-ok began his administration in 1966 that would consist of major infrastructural development policies such as the underground passages on Sejong-daero and Myeongdong, vehicular overpasses, expanding and paving main roads, Hangang Development Project, opening of Namsan Tunnel 1 and 2, 400 apartment buildings, Yeongdong zones 1 and 2, Hwayang, Mangu District, Siheung, Sillim District, and other large district reorganization projects.[140] These large infrastructural projects would earn him the nickname of the "Bulldozer Mayor." As one of his first redevelopment projects to clean, modernize, and reorganize the city, Kim Hyon-ok commissions Kim Swoo Geun to propose a project for the kilometer long strip of land in order to clear the shantytown.[141] At the time Kim Swoo Geun was regarded as a star architect among the first generation of Korean international architects. Having graduated from Tokyo University in 1958, Kim Swoo Geun was influenced by Kenzo Tange who in the coming years would introduce the avant-garde movement of Metabolism. This became an opportunity to test ideas and concepts for megastructures through the development of Seun Sangga in 1967 in that kilometer long strip of land. This project represented a new attitude toward organizing the city not only through large interventions of a singular building, but also through an integration with infrastructure. Due to the need for construction on city owned land, Seun Sangga would integrate pedestrian decks at an upper level while maintaining vehicular roads at a ground level. Its massive scale aimed at housing over 2,000 households, which competed with the scale of a single apartment block.

From 1966 to 1979, 34 new apartment buildings were constructed not following the apartment complex logic but instead as singular buildings with mixed uses that formed their own contained neighborhood. Fifteen of these were named Sangga 상가 (store), representing the new shopping arcade typology integrated to housing in order to offer all the amenities within one site. The appearance of these megaforms begin to alter the urban landscape and composition of the city as these autonomous forms re-define edges within the historic core producing a new island typology of singular buildings acting as entire blocks. Unlike the mega structural logic of the Smithsons or the Metabolist, the ones constructed in Seoul remained as stand-alone objects rather than systems of urbanization. Due to the lack of land and the reliance of the government on using the air rights over streets, these structures originally conceptualized as megastructures would in a way function more like megaforms, in the definition described by Frampton.[142] They would have their own inner logic, and their monumental scale would separate them from the rest of the fabric defining the urban landscape.

Superblock

During the 1960s a drastic population increase from 2.4 million in 1960 to 5.5 million people by 1970[143] forced the city to produce a series of planning strategies that could cope with the speed of growth. This pressure expanded the city to Yeongdong (south of the river). Gangnam had already been incorporated as part of Seoul in 1963 and presented the new frontier for expansion as Yongsan and Yeongdeungpo had begun their urbanization during the Japanese colonial period. Gangnam was developed in two phases through land-reclamation projects. Yeongdong I was developed in 1968 and consisted mainly of Seocho. Yeongdong II followed in 1971 after the Hannam bridge and Gyeongbu Expressway opened in 1969.[144]

Inha Jung defines three planning methods that were implemented at the time: concentric expansion of urban boundaries, subdivision of urban space based on the neighborhood unit theory, and development of large apartment complexes.[145] The second and third methods led to the development of the apartment block (as previously mentioned) and the creation of the superblock typology.

At the time, urban planning was a fairly new discipline with the first department in Urban Studies being founded in 1967. Planning was led through the advisory of three groups, the Korean Planners Association, the Korean Engineering Consultants Corporation, and the Housing, Urban, and Regional Planning Institute.[146] The first group was guided by Byung Joo Park, an academic who would develop a modernist conceptual plan of Seoul in 1966, and later the masterplan for Yeouido and Jamsil. The second group would be led by Kim Swoo Geun, who sought to introduce visionary Metabolist ideas through Seun Sangga and the plan for Yeouido. The third group, on the other hand, was led by Oswald Nagler who had studied under Josep Lluis Sert at Harvard and had been invited to Korea by the Asian foundation to review the state of urbanization. Unlike Park's functionalist modernist approach, or

Figure 3.6 Commercial boulevard separating superblocks in Gangnam.

Geun's Metabolist agenda, Nagler introduced a linear system model of urbanization and Clarence Perry's concept for the neighborhood unit, which was based on the population that one elementary school could sustain, as a block type. Each neighborhood unit was self-contained in a 500–800 m width. These would be produced through the understanding of the minimum dwelling unit and its aggregation to form a collective. The ideas were presented in the HURPI's exhibition of 1967, and would become highly influential in the development of the superblock typology.[147]

Nagler proposed a linear system of urbanization after reviewing the 1966 plan of Seoul, which followed Abercrombie's plan of London.[148] The 1966 plan defined a concentric city with a nucleus and subcenters that produced a decentralization to Yongsan, Yeongdeungpo, and Gangnam.[149] Nagler saw the concentric plan as a limited model of expansion as the bounding circles would inevitably become larger, covering longer distances whenever the city needed to grow. Instead, Nagler favored a linear system that allowed for flexibility in correlation to the necessary infrastructure. With the pressure of time, the linear model is dismissed and the 1966 plan to urbanize Gangnam is maintained. Planned by the Korean Planners Association, the 1966 plan already defined the street networks and block partitions following the subcenter layout of the 20 year plan. The grid pattern and riverside road were appropriated from the Manhattan model, but adjusted to blocks divided with 50 m wide boulevards averaging 670 m × 680 m in size.[150] Jung notes that presumably that the block partition in the 1966 plan was in reference to the distance from Jongno to Gwanghwamun, approximately 570 m. Once the plan was directly administered to the area, it ran into topographical and soil issues that required modifications of block size and alignments as the grid adjusted to the terrain. While the plan of 1966 called for five gridded sections, the topographical readjustments produced 8 segments as they exist today. The rapid implementation of the plan lacked details on population redistribution, land readjustment, and projected for a population of 5.6 million after 20 years.[151] Hence, the intention of producing these superblocks was to be able to develop the land quickly by distributing these large parcels that could induce irregular subdivisions in the interior of the block. Different zoning codes, and FAR regulations between the perimeter of the blocks and the interior of the blocks, resulted in a unique condition of confining a high-density, low-rise, pedestrian environment in the interior of the block, while the perimeter held larger buildings, high-rises with commercial use. These superblocks can be understood as urban villages with a commercial perimeter wall of high-rises.

Globalization Period (1980–2002)

Tower Block

Since the Basic Urban Plan of 1966, the master planning of Seoul had been scrambling to keep up with the rapid growth in population while maintaining an organized spatial structure with one main center and five subcenters. While this plan targeted a population of five million by 1985, the target was met and surpassed in the early 1970s. In 1970, the Modification of the "Basic Urban Plan" revised the target to 7.5 million by 1991. To ease the strains of the historic center as a Central Business District, Yeouido was introduced as a new business center. The plan was revised yet again in 1972 and again in 1978 where the multiple nuclei model was introduced with a target of 9.45 million people by 2001.[152]

By this time, Seoul had reached 8.5 million people, with a strong middle class, large corporations, and diversified industries. In an effort to present Seoul as a global city, Park Chung Hee began discussing the possibility of hosting the Olympics in Seoul during the 1970s until his assassination in 1979. Seoul would eventually be awarded the bid in 1981 to host the 1986 Asian Games and the 1988 Summer Olympic games.[153] This inspired

Figure 3.7 Lotte Tower as a conceptual vertical city forms a tower block.

a beautification agenda for the city and the urban redevelopment plans that had reached an impasse were quickly revived in order to present Seoul to the world as a modern capital city.

The city government passed the Urban Redevelopment Act in 1982 after establishing a five year urban development plan.[154] For the purpose of financing, eminent domain is granted to private corporations and stereo replotting is integrated as a methodology to reintegrate the divided land into a vertical share of ownership. The FAR ratio is purposely increased within the historic core to 1000% and taxes on transfers, acquisition, and registration were removed ensuring profitability for the developer in return for the beautification project for the city center in preparation for the global events.[155] The ensured profitability of developing in the central district became attractive to large corporations, and was also used as an excuse for the city to redevelop inner city slums. The city approved 70 redevelopment projects and focused their attention on Euljiro in the central district and Tehran-ro in Gangnam.

The Korean economy flourished, driven by low oil prices, low international interest rates and the weak Korean won against the Japanese yen. The demand for office space in Seoul skyrocketed, which further boosted urban redevelopment. For the years between 1983 and 1986, urban redevelopment programs were approved in 76 districts, and the trend remained in place until the Olympics in 1988.[156]

The Olympic efforts of beautification had the effect of promoting architecture of modernity and globalization in Seoul, resulting in the emergence of corporate international style tower blocks and commercial deep block typologies. The corporate tower became an emblem of industrial prowess, capital power and a strong labor force. Already the modern skyscraper had been introduced in Seoul in 1970 when Kim Jung Up designed the Samil Building inspired by the Seagrams Building of Mies van der Rohe.[157] One-hundred and ten meters tall 31-story Samil Building would dominate the skyline as the tallest building in Seoul until the Lotte Hotel Seoul was built in 1979 also within the central historic core.

While these two towers became modern landmarks in the Central Business District, two more symbolic towers were built during the pre-olympics preparation and modernization. The 63 Building was completed in 1985 in Yeouido, and the Trade Tower was completed in 1988 in Gangnam marking the importance of these two subcenters as centers of commerce.

The 63 Building, originally the DLI 63 Building, would become the headquarters of Daehan Life Insurance and the tallest building in Korea.[158] Standing at 249 m, with 60 floors aboveground and 3 underground, the building offers an array of programs open to the public such as a shopping mall, theater, aquarium, convention center, and banquet hall in the lower floors. An art gallery and high-end restaurants were placed in the upper floors.

While the 63 Building showcased singular corporate success, the Trade Tower is part of the new global capital agenda that sought to provide infrastructure for global trade and commerce conceptualized as a premier business town. Built for the Korea International Trade Association, the Trade Tower was designed primarily as an office building, standing at 228 m with 54 floors, that forms part of the World Trade Center Seoul, which was also established in 1988.[159]

Made up of mostly small and medium-sized companies dealing in trade, logistics, and IT, as well as global corporations and foreign trade organizations, the Office Tower offers these businesses international recognition, business planning, trade information, convenient transportation, various facilities and advanced services that are unique to the World Trade Center Seoul.[160]

Although verticalism arrived in Seoul as a product of density policies adopted for apartment developments that could accommodate the increasing population in Seoul, the inception of buildings like the Trade Tower or DLI 63 Building represent a new condition for verticalism as an architectural typological island. These buildings would encapsulate an urban microcosm within them. Joseph Fenton would describe this typology as monoliths in the city in his 1985 Hybrid Architecture Pamphlet.[161]

> Monolith hybrids are inherently products of the industrialized Twentieth Century city. The impact of their monumental scale on the spirit of the city is substantial. These highly present buildings often concentrate an encyclopedia of metropolitan life within a single building block. Their self-generating symbolism also supersedes the simplistic equation of form and function. In the modern city, the monolith hybrid, with its efficient accommodation of the most extreme functions, has displayed greatest versatility.[162]

In this description of the skyscraper as a "monolith hybrid," Fenton is referring to the concept of metropolitan architecture that can be condensed through O. M. Ungers's manifesto for "the city within a city." While Ungers conceptualized the formation of urban islands through the fusion of multiple typologies into an urban cluster, Koolhaas would explore this condition through the interiority of a single building as explained in his 1977 essay, "Life in the Metropolis or the Culture of Congestion."[163] For Koolhaas, the skyscraper represents the possibility to multiply the same parcel of ground vertically, and allow for non-relatable programs to layer on independent floors one on top of another, aided through the use of technology. Through this article a few postulations were made toward interpreting metropolitan architecture as an insular architecture. First, "the building is an accumulation of privacies."[164] The fact that each floor is a conceptual duplication of the parcel, implies that multiple iterations of architectural interventions can be achieved within a single building. Second, the location of the building is irrelevant as it is an autonomous setting. The 100 Story Building project from 1911, which Koolhaas uses to illustrate as an example, integrates industry, business, and living while also including retail, markets, and entertainment. Aside from offering all the functions of the city within one building, its HVAC system could regulate the temperature and humidity to emulate different climate environments.

"The building has become a laboratory for emotional and intellectual adventure; the fact that it is implanted in Manhattan has become – almost – immaterial."[165] Third, the building can be used as an instrument of density, a "constructivist social condenser"[166] that achieves the effects of metropolitan events. The proximity between disparate programs produces the potential for unprogrammed events to occur, as canonically explained through the aid of the 9th floor plan of the New York Athletic Club where naked boxers eat oysters in a locker room.

Through these postulations, metropolitan architecture proposes an architecture of autonomy through the abstraction of the city within a building. The most emblematic example in Seoul is the Lotte World Tower completed in 2017 in Jamsil. Currently, the fifth tallest in the world, this supertall building stands at 556 m and 123 stories.[167] First planned in 1998 with the aim of becoming a new icon in the city, attracting almost 3 million visitors and creating 20,000 jobs. Construction began in 2010. While it stands as a corporate emblem, it is designed as a vertical city by KPF Associates as an urban response, conceptualized as the ultimate unit of urbanity. "It is inevitable that globalization and urbanization will persist, raising issues regarding population growth and urban density. The supertall tower and 'vertical cities' created in response to these conditions present a solution."[168]

Deep Block

Paired with the autonomous vertical city, a horizontal typology would also be conceived. Buildings like the World Trade Tower and Lotte Hotel that

Figure 3.8 Wangsimni station as a deep block.

produced micro-cities would also build singular shell horizontal buildings at their base or adjacent. These massive box-like buildings would cover an entire city block in order to incorporate all the amenities and services that would also compliment the towers. These became deep block typologies. Often associated with commercial retail malls, this architectural island typology is referenced by Koolhaas in S,M,L,XL as "Bigness or the Problem of Large" within globalizing "Generic City."[169]

Through terms like "Bigness" and "Generic City," Koolhaas depicted the banal condition of cities that the project of urbanization had created. The "Generic City" described the process by which the repetitive development had propagated across the globe generating a familiarity in the construct of the city. This phenomenon is extensively explored as well by Keller Esterling in her book *Extrastatecraft* where she describes how these extra-large commercial developments are becoming the infrastructure for globalization as their model is repeated throughout the developing world.[170] "Bigness" described the scale jump needed for these new commercial developments. These big projects produced an architecture of exterior shells that challenged the over-scaled production of space. At this scale, architecture competes with the scale of infrastructure as architecture is reduced to a shell condition for programs and events to be plugged in independently from the shell. Due to the scale and the possibility of enclosing a metropolitan environment, the deep block typology can be understood as an urban island.

In Seoul, this typology is characteristic of the mega-department stores which began to appear through the competition of three *Chaebols*,[171] Lotte, Hyundai, and Samsung. The first department store in Korea, Mitsukoshi, was originally started during the Japanese occupation in 1906.[172] This would become part of the Samsung group and change its name to Shinsegae in 1963.[173] Its main building in Myeongdong would expand to occupy an entire city block. Lotte Department Store would also open in Myeongdong in 1979 connected to the Lotte Hotel Seoul tower.[174] The Hyundai Department store would follow in 1985 in Apgujeong.[175] These three would present a model for a self-contained commercial city block. While still mono-functional, due to their size, the department stores would begin offering a variety of environments that would eventually morph into megamalls found primarily in Seoul at main train stations. As explained by Abalos and Herreros in their essay on Hybrids, the interiorization of public space is intrinsically linked to public transportation due to the heavy flow of pedestrian traffic, which drives these commercial hubs. Shinsegae, for example, would become part of the development of Central City in Gangnam. This is an infrastructural and commercial development consisting of a bus terminal, department store, shopping mall, hotel, Megabox movie theater, and Bandi & Lunis bookstore, of which Shinsegae Group owns a 60.02% share as of 2012.[176] The growth of development between the different stakeholders would occupy a megablock of 350 m × 720 m, yet the entire site works as a singular interior space composed of large shells. Similarly, Lotte Department Stores would expand with Seoul Station, Yeongdeungpo Station, and Cheongnyangni Station. After opening the Hyundai Department Store in Apgujeong in 1985, a second branch would expand the brand at the World Trade Center in 1988 within a block of 300 m × 650 m that also houses the COEX (Convention and Exhibition Center), COEX Mall, and Starfield Mall.[177]

Cultural Industry Period (2002–present)

Cultural Block

While globalization had been fomented with the 1986 Asian games and 1988 Olympic games, a new agenda for cultural identity started shaping economic and urban policy toward the end of the 20th century. "In addition, the

Figure 3.9 The tectonic consistency and historical heritage of Bukchon make it a cultural block.

globalization policy set in motion in 1995 by the government of Kim Young Sam required the government to reshape its cultural policy toward enhancement of international cultural exchange."[178] Globalization had brought Seoul to the world stage, and the 1996 selection for Korea and Japan to co-host the 2002 World Cup would provide a new globalization platform to present Seoul as a 21st-century city.

Up to the decade of the 1990s, Korea had cultural identity policies that mainly promoted the arts through the establishment of laws, institutions, and funds to support the cultural sector. Yet globalization would eventually require a stronger cultural exchange with foreign nations. Haksoon Yim points out that this led to a duality between Korea trying to promote a unifying cultural identity that showcases Korean heritage and culture while at the same time, a globalization policy that paradoxically would homogenize the cultural traits. Yet, a strong cultural identity would serve as a means of competitiveness in the global scene.

Jieheerah Yun defines this new agenda as a "cultural city discourse."[179] A discourse that emerged as a transition from a city propelled by an industrial economy into a post-industrial information age. Guided by studies conducted in 2001 and 2002 by the Seoul Institute, a shift of focus into a cultural industry was necessary as a way to generate foreign investment in Seoul. Based on the 1985 European Capital of Culture Programme, a new economy based on culture should transform the "hard city," which was a product of industrialization, into a "soft city," one guided by a better quality of life, appreciative of traditional cultural values. "The cultural city discourse proposed a new set of urban renaissance projects in order to recover from the ills of modernization and restore the balance between material growth and appreciation of the non-economic aspects of life."[180]

As a way of promoting cultural exchange with foreign nations through urban planning, Seoul designates 15 global zones within the city. These consist of four global business zones, six global villages and five global cultural exchange zones as a way to provide comfort for living, conducting business and education for foreigners in Seoul.[181]

Targeting foreigners in Seoul, the villages would group areas with large populations of cultural enclaves such as Dongbu Ichon for the Japanese community, Seorae Village for the French community, UN Village in Hannam dong for international embassy residents, for example. Heavy commercial areas such as Itaewon, Myeongdong, Dongdaemun, and Namdaemun would also get designated as cultural exchange zones. These designation would form artificial urban islands of made-up boundaries, yet, these zones form agglomerations of likewise typologies that produce what Maki would classify as "group forms."[182] For Maki, when discussing issues of collective form, the group form is one that has a sequential growth, with consistent tectonics, not by the same author, with an open-ended structure (meaning it can grow or shrink indiscriminately). The Bukchon Hanok Village in Seoul for example, represents the perfect example for these cultural zones becoming cultural islands. Through government incentives, the restoration of Hanoks in Bukchon at the beginning of the 2000s transformed the North Village into a tourist attraction. The vernacular composition of these mono-functional buildings was adapted into restaurants, cafes, private residences, and galleries, drastically different from the corporate skyscrapers outside of the district.

Podium Block

The apartment typology has dominated the housing scene since its emergence in 1962 with the Mapo Apartment Complex by the now Korea Land and Housing Corporation. The role for the KLHC in the adoption of mass housing is uncontested as it secured 132,232,000 m² in Hwagok-dong in 1965 and during the 1970s constructed 7,906 housing units in Banpo and 19,180 in Jamsil

Figure 3.10 The commercial podium creates a new ground for apartment towers forming a podium block.

alone.[183] The land-reclamation method for housing which established apartment blocks as urban islands, also facilitated the mass production of housing as a repeated model. As further housing was needed during the fast-growing decades of the 1960s to the 1980s, mass housing was built in a similar manner by a few construction companies commissioned by the government. While the target was simply to fulfill a quota for family housing needed, inevitably, branding became strategic for the construction companies to differentiate their housing among what seemed as cookie cutter development of housing throughout Seoul. While the model of construction was repeated among the different developments, the brand reflected a consumer's lifestyle. "When asked about their priorities when choosing an apartment, 51 percent said that the brand is the top factor if other options are similar."[184]

By the 1990s and 2000s the major construction companies like Lotte, Samsung, Daelim, GS, Daewoo, Hyundai, Posco, Kumho, CJ, SK, KCC, among a few others, had established their recognizable brands, yet started targeting new lifestyles and luxury consumers through the launch of new brands that would deviate from the traditional apartment block model. Lotte Engineering & Construction Co introduced Lotte Castle in 1999, GS Engineering & Construction introduced the Xi brand in 2002, Daelim Industrial Co introduced Arco in 2013, Daewoo E&C introduced Prugio Summit in 2014, Hyundai Engineering & Construction Co introduced the H in 2015, and Lotte Engineering & Construction Co introduced the LE-EL in 2019. The scarcity of land and new lifestyles that demanded a higher integration of services within the apartment complex resulted in a new architectural island typology – the podium block.

The typical podium block consists of a commercial podium that occupies the majority of the block (based on the allowable building coverage ratio), and high-rise apartment buildings on top of the podium (based on FAR). The podium serves as a new ground for the buildings on top, hence one is architecturally independent of the other in an almost live version of Koolhaas's "The City of the Captive Globe" from 1972.[185]

Hilberseimer had already presented a model of urbanization through the podium in his proposal for Berlin's "Vertical City" in 1924. In this case, the podium and tower represented a congruent unit that was meant to be repeated, producing an expandable grid. Unlike the Vertical City, The City of The Captive Globe presented the podium as the repeatable part, which provided a new ground for any architecture to be placed on top, independently. Despite some of these projects being conflicting oppositions or architectural manifestos from different eras, they can exist as independent islands, separated and contained through the limits of the podium.

For Seoul, the podium typology exists as smaller developments that occupy entire blocks. Unlike the deep block, or the superblock, the podium block occupies smaller parcels. Brands like Acro and Lotte Castle have been able to develop in denser areas in the city center through this strategy.

Application of Architectural Typological Islands

Nine architectural typological islands have been identified as repeated blocks throughout Seoul. These are the political form block, iconic form block, apartment block, megaform block, superblock, tower block, deep block, podium block, and cultural block. Although these block typologies are meant to highlight architecture as the defining factor for bounded subunits, road infrastructure further accentuates these islands. In Gangnam, for example, 50 m boulevards separate superblocks in their peripheries. Other building typologies not described in this research, such as villas, IT Towers, and Officetel Towers, may sometimes find themselves bounded by road infrastructure rather than through a group form. These undefined mixed groupings may be read as islands as well by contrast to the surrounding well defined typological islands.

The theory of the urban jungle as explained by Kipnis[186] (adopted from Carl Chu) can also be applied for the remaining context in-between the nine islands. The "jungle" relies on the grouping of multiple species, paradoxically forming congruence through variation.

The understanding of the different typological groupings allows for mappings of Seoul to be produced as a series of color-coded blobs (graphically borrowing from Abercrombie's potato plan of London[187]) that represent architectural typological islands. These mappings describe an architectural qualitative reading as opposed to an infrastructural one. For example, comparing the Central Business District (CBD) to Gangnam, one can see the density and variety of islands in the main core, rather than the homogeneity of apartment blocks and superblocks in Gangnam. The density of cultural blocks in the CBD are also a reflection of the cultural identity policies, which means that the quality of urban space found in these islands will most likely consist of historic areas, and tourist destinations. The comparison of the different districts through this mapping also reveals a general sense of density. The CBD has the least amount of apartments, while Gangnam, and Jamsil have the most.

While this methodology of mapping is abstract, through further analysis of a specific architectural island typology, sublayers of quantitative and qualitative information can be generated.

While the historical background of the architectural island typologies explains their initial formations, and the definition of the nine islands, some blocks can adapt and change over time, yet the definitions of the typologies stay the same. For example, in the contemporary makeup of Seoul, the political form block is found in university campuses rather than in royal grounds. The royal grounds became public grounds for cultural amenities such as parks and museums after the colonial period, and today they are protected as cultural heritage making them act more like cultural blocks. Instead, university campuses follow more closely the

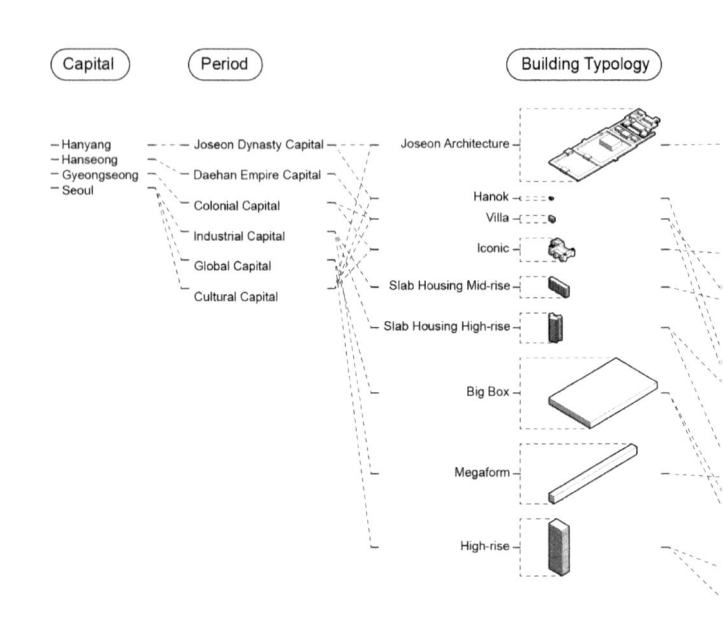

Figure 3.11 Different periods in the history of Seoul formed specific building typologies that led to particular block typologies.

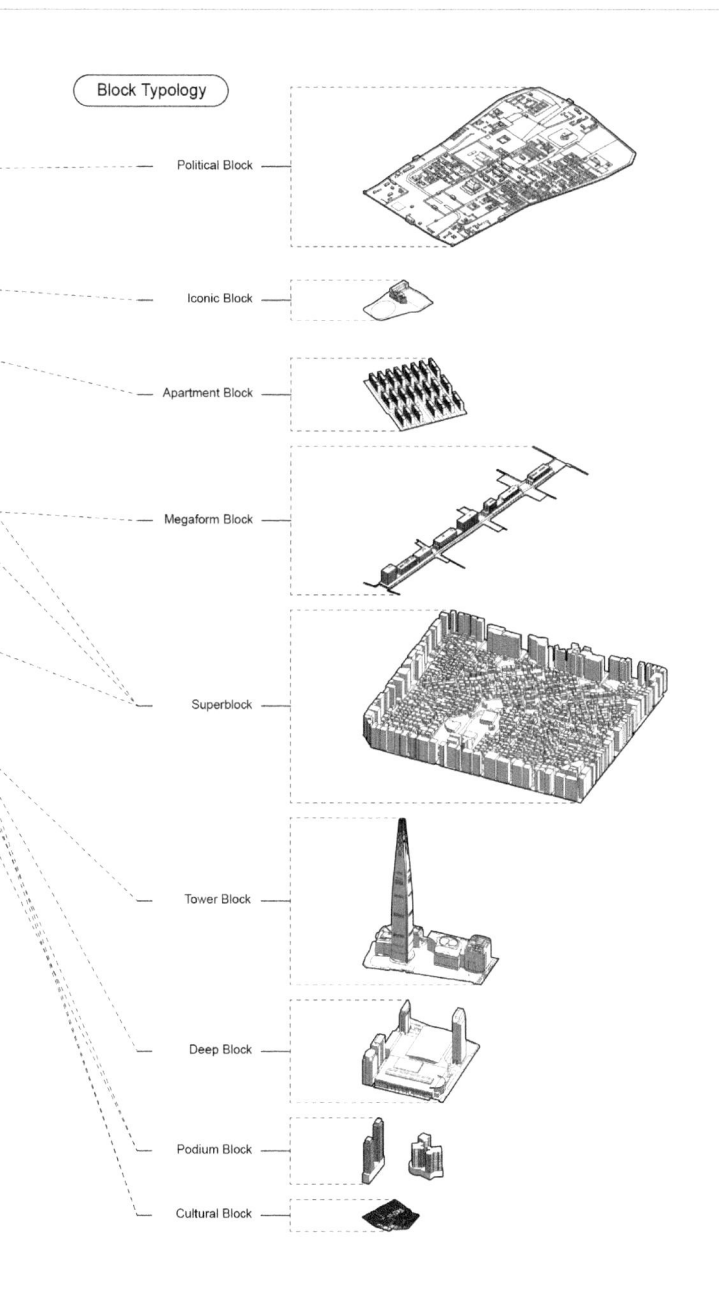

Figure 3.11 (Continued)

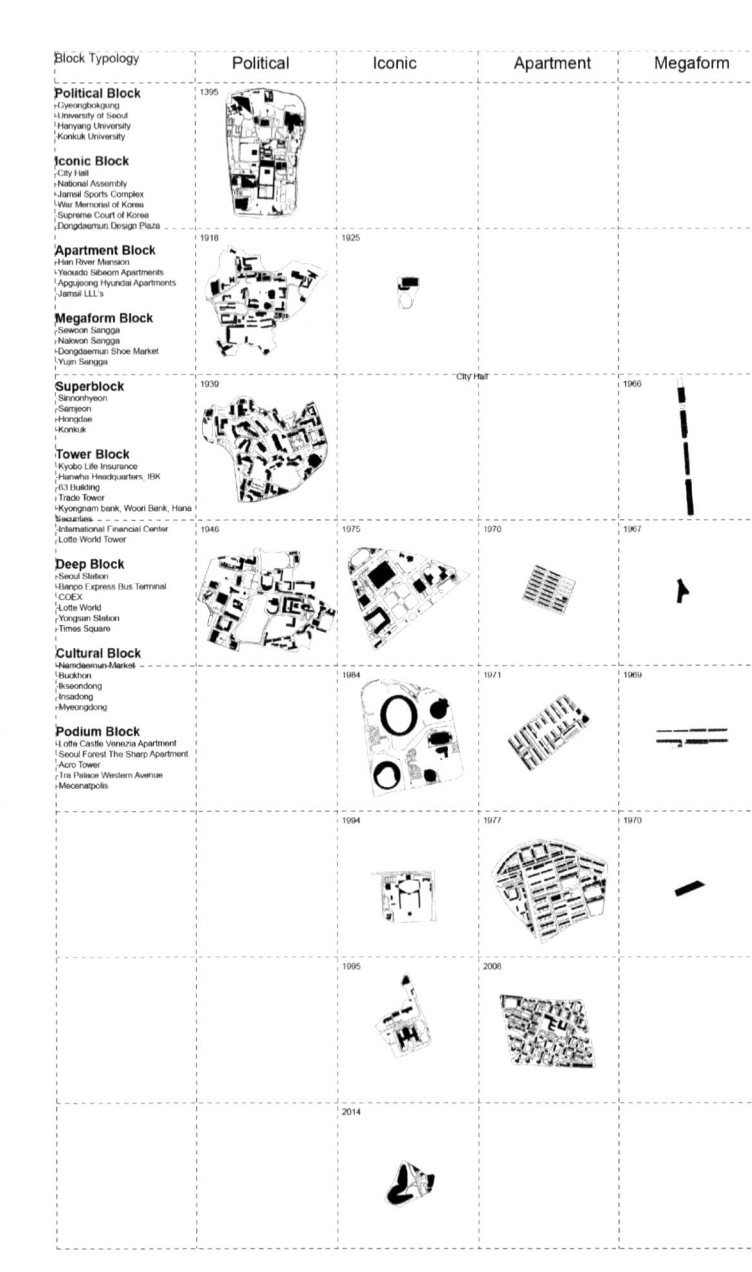

Figure 3.12 Examples of typological blocks.

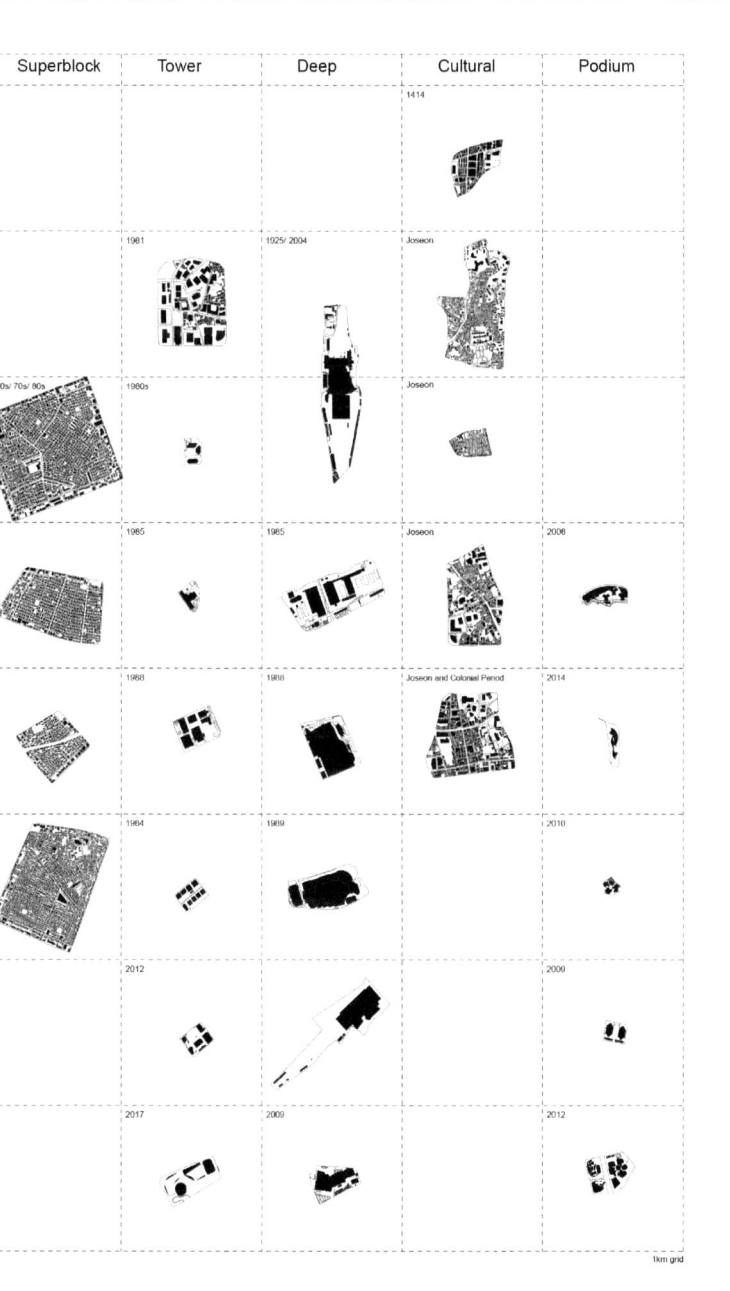

Superblock	Tower	Deep	Cultural	Podium

Figure 3.12 (Continued)

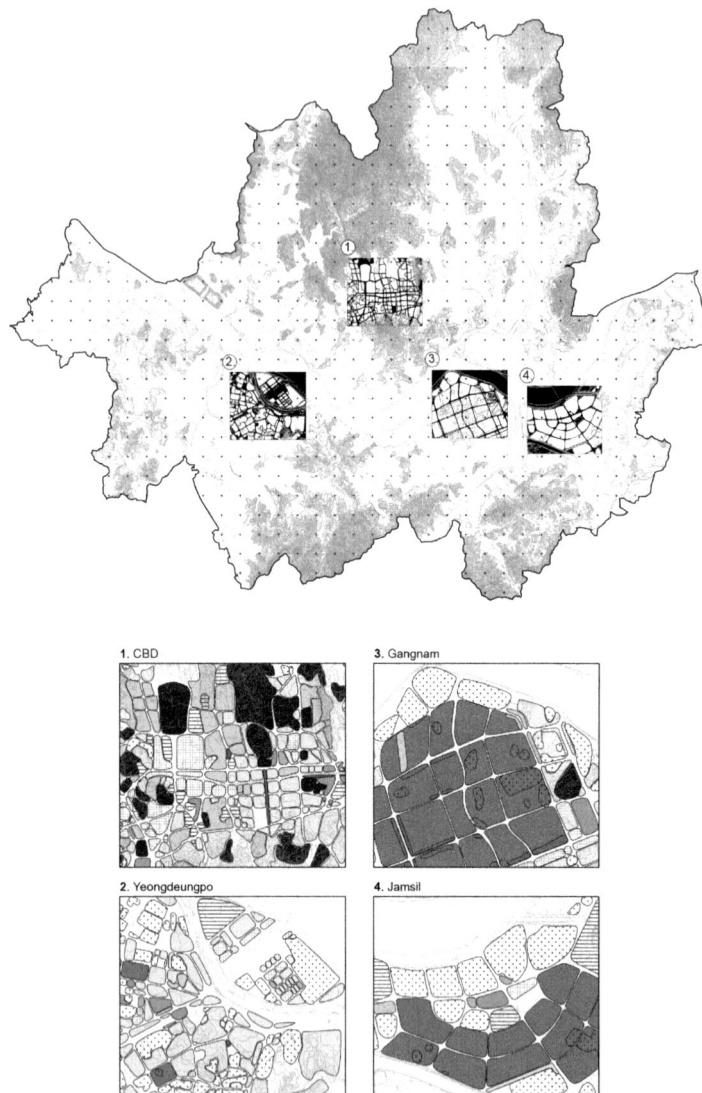

Figure 3.13 Typological Potato Plan for different urban cores of Seoul.

original definition of political form blocks; physically bounded grounds with their own urban structure within them. These campuses follow a similar suburban campus strategy despite being within a dense urban fabric. The universities presented bounded low-density compounds that separate themselves with the use of walls and gates and formed their own edu-towns.

The university campuses, despite being from different institutions, follow the same typology of block. Though the student populations vary from 10,000 to 30,000, the floor area ratio (FAR), building coverage ratio (BCR), amenities, building types, and facilities are fairly similar, indicating that the quality of space is similar in all of these blocks.

A subcategory of the same block typology can be generated by separating them by year of development. By showing that typological blocks have different sublayers, it can add to the complexity of data that can be generated per block type.

Due to the development cycles in Seoul of building replacement every 30 years, different generations of apartments present different properties based on current demographics, construction technology, lifestyle research, among other factors. For example, apartment block typologies from the past decade offer underground parking to provide more playgrounds and common recreational spaces at ground level between the buildings. A retail low-rise periphery building may surround the complex with convenience stores, pharmacies, fruit markets, banks, cafes, medical centers, daycare/kindergarten, among other services and amenities in order to service the mono-functional apartments.

The heat mapping of the apartment blocks per year of development reveals another layer of information with regard to the architectural quality of space generated by apartment buildings since apartments built between the 1960s and 1980s focused on quantity and have the same layout while apartment blocks in the 1990s and toward the present offer more amenities. This might also be indicative of where the next development might occur as most blocks have a 30 year lifespan.

Typological blocks can also be analyzed for appropriations, meaning how humans occupy the built space beyond its intended design and understand how certain typologies produce urban fabrics that allow for specific appropriations. This directly correlates to the spatial quality associated with the typology that builds up that particular island. Hongdae and Sinsa-dong, for example, share the same typology; they are both *cultural superblocks* (developed as superblocks but were designated as touristic centers). They both follow the generic composition of a superblock, a high-rise perimeter with a fine grain low-rise interior. While these two blocks are not part of the global zones, they are considered cultural blocks for tourism. These are both high-density commercial areas with high pedestrian traffic. Due to the high price of real estate, Hongdae exhibits commercial appropriations of the in-between spaces for micro-shops, retail extensions, and additional access to the back or upper floor in order to gain more retail area inside. Although the maximum allowable building coverage ratio is 60%, through the appropriation of the in-between space, the BCR increases to 77%. Sinsa-dong exhibits the same properties with the occupation of the in-between in order to increase the retail density.

The tendency for islands to behave similarly allows for an abstract architectural overview assuming the analysis of case studies for each island typology can be interpreted with an allowance for variability.

As Seoul keeps on developing, the construction of islands keeps on homogenizing the urban framework replacing "jungle" islands for typological ones. This process of urban transformation reinforces the archipelago reading of Seoul and facilitates the interpretation of the city as architecture. Since the typological islands are bounded forms, their agglomeration clarifies what may seem as urban sprawl is in fact a city form. The megacity therefore does not require one singular form but a collection of bounded architectural subunits, which have been categorized as architectural typological islands. There are some key points to be noted from this chapter. The repetition of the same typology in a group form produces a typological island. In this research, nine typological islands were identified. Each typological island has specific spatial, quantifiable characteristics with regard to the built environment that are produced by the building type. The building type also has qualitative properties that could be investigated through case studies for each typology. Understanding the qualitative and quantitative characteristics of a case study allows for a quick reading of the city based on urban spaces (typological islands) that can be mapped out as a "potato plan." This mapping methodology adds layers of information missing from a more traditional figure-ground mapping method, which is more commonly used for studying urban sprawl.

Notes

1 Maki, Fumihiko. *Investigations in Collective Form*. St Louis: Washington University, School of Architecture, 1964.
2 Center for International Affairs. "Seoul – 4.1 Population Growth and Expansion of the Urban Center." *Seoul – 4.1 Population Growth and Expansion of the Urban Center – CefiaWiki*, 19 Jan. 2017, http://cefia.aks.ac.kr:84/index.php?title=Seoul_-_4.1_Population_Growth_and_Expansion_of_the_Urban_Center.
3 Ibid.
4 Ibid.
5 Statistics Korea. "Kosis Korean Statistical Information Service." *Statistical Database Population Census*, https://kosis.kr/eng/statisticsList/statisticsListIndex.do?menuId=M_01_01&vwcd=MT_ETITLE&parmTabId=M_01_01#content-group.
6 Ibid.
7 Ibid.
8 Ghosh, Iman. "70 Years of Urban Growth in 1 Dazzling Infographic." *World Economic Forum*, 3 Sept. 2019, www.weforum.org/agenda/2019/09/mapped-the-dramatic-global-rise-of-urbanization-1950-2020/.
9 United Nations, Department of Economic and Social Affairs Population Division. *World Urbanization Prospects the 2018 Revision*. United Nations, 2019, pp. 1–103.

10 Ritchie, Hannah, and Max Roser. "Urbanization." *Our World in Data*, 13 June 2018, https://ourworldindata.org/urbanization.

11 *Global Human Settlement – Atlas of the Human Planet 2016 Overview – European Commission*, 6 July 2016, https://ghsl.jrc.ec.europa.eu/documents/Atlas_2016.pdf

12 Angel, Schlomo. "[Re]Form: New Investigations in Urban Form, Panel 2." *YouTube*, Harvard Graduate School of Design, 26 Sept. 2018, https://youtu.be/a2RaiAORKks.

13 "Atlas of Urban Expansion." *Atlas of Urban Expansion – Cities*, 2016, www.atlasofurbanexpansion.org/data.

14 Züger, Mirjam, and Kees Christiaanse. *The Potato PLAN Collection: 40 Cities Through the Lens of Patrick Abercrombie*. Rotterdam: nai010 Publishers, 2018.

15 Ibid., p. 8.

16 Ungers, Oswald M., et al. *Cities Within the City: Proposals by the Sommer Akademie for Berlin*. Ithaca: Cornell University, 1978, pp. 82–97.

17 Ibid.

18 Koolhaas, Rem. *Delirious New York: A Retroactive Manifesto for Manhattan*. New York: Monacelli, 1994.

19 Rowe, Colin, and Fred Koetter. *Collage City*. Basel: Birkhäuser, 2009.

20 Kang, Hong-bin, editor. *Seoul Museum of History: Places and Memories*. Seoul: Seoul Museum of History, 2013, p. 9.

21 Annals of King Taejo. *Chapter 6, 13th Day of 8th Month, 1394*. Seoul: Seoul Museum of History.

22 Ibid.

23 Annals of King Taejo. *Chapter 6, 13th Day of 8th Month, 1394*. Seoul: Seoul Museum of History.

24 Henry, Todd A. *Assimilating Seoul: Japanese Rule and the Politics of Public Space in Colonial Korea, 1910–1945*. Berkeley: University of California Press, 2016, p. 23.

25 Kang, Hong-bin, editor. *Seoul Museum of History: Places and Memories*. Seoul: Seoul Museum of History, 2013, p. 15.

26 Kang, Hong-bin, editor. *History of Seoul: Seoul Museum of History, Places and Memories*. Seoul: Seoul Museum of History, 2014. P. 10

27 Ibid., p. 14.

28 Kang, Hong-bin, editor. *Seoul Museum of History: Places and Memories*. Seoul: Seoul Museum of History, 2013, p. 14.

29 Jeon, Wu-Yong. *The Soul City Wall: Walking the History of Seoul*. Seoul: The Seoul Institute, 2018, p. 44.

30 Ibid., p. 46.

31 Ibid., p. 43.

32 Ibid., p. 46.

33 Ibid., p. 42.

34 Ibid., p. 47.

35 Ibid., p. 44.

36 Ibid.

37 Henry, Todd A. *Assimilating Seoul: Japanese Rule and the Politics of Public Space in Colonial Korea, 1910–1945*. Berkeley: University of California Press, 2016, p. 23.

38 Kang, Hong-bin, editor. *Seoul Museum of History: Places and Memories*. Seoul: Seoul Museum of History, 2013, p. 40.
39 Ibid., p. 42.
40 Jeon, Wu-Yong. *The Soul City Wall: Walking the History of Seoul*. Seoul: The Seoul Institute, 2018, p. 6.
41 Kang, Hong-bin. *History of Seoul: Places and Memories*. Seoul: Seoul Museum of History, 2014, p. 20.
42 Kang, Hong-bin, editor. *Seoul Museum of History: Places and Memories*. Seoul: Seoul Museum of History, 2013, p. 42.
43 Ibid., p. 40.
44 Henry, Todd A. *Assimilating Seoul: Japanese Rule and the Politics of Public Space in Colonial Korea, 1910–1945*. Berkeley: University of California Press, 2016, p. 23.
45 Kang, Hong-bin, editor. *Seoul Museum of History: Places and Memories*. Seoul: Seoul Museum of History, 2013, p. 48.
46 Ibid., p. 88.
47 Ibid., p. 89.
48 Henry, Todd A. *Assimilating Seoul: Japanese Rule and the Politics of Public Space in Colonial Korea, 1910–1945*. Berkeley: University of California Press, 2016, p. 23.
49 Aureli, Pier Vittorio. *The Possibility of an Absolute Architecture*. Cambridge, MA: The MIT Press, 2011.
50 Kang, Hong-bin, editor. *Seoul Museum of History: Places and Memories*. Seoul: Seoul Museum of History, 2013, p. 12.
51 Seoul Metropolitan Government. *Into SEOUL*. Seoul: Seoul Metropolitan Government, 2020, p. 41.
52 Ibid.
53 Kang, Hong-bin, editor. *Seoul Museum of History: Places and Memories*. Seoul: Seoul Museum of History, 2013, p. 20.
54 "About Deoksugung Palace." *Deoksugung*, Cultural Heritage Administration, http://deoksugung.go.kr/en/c/about/2.
55 Ibid., p. 36.
56 Cultural Heritage Administration of Korea. *Main Palace: Center of Power, Politics, Economy, and Culture*. Daejeon: Cultural Heritage Administration of Korea, 2011, p. 1.
57 Song, In-ho. *Maps of Old Seoul*. Seoul: Seoul Museum of History, 2016, p. 19.
58 Ibid., p. 63.
59 Ibid., p. 86.
60 Ibid., p. 31.
61 Ibid.
62 Ibid., p. 89.
63 Kim, Joochul, and Sang-Chuel Choe. *Seoul: The Making of a Metropolis*. Chichester: Wiley, 1997, p. 61.
64 Ibid., p. 83.
65 Kang, Hong-bin, editor. *Seoul Museum of History: Places and Memories*. Seoul: Seoul Museum of History, 2013, pp. 60–61.
66 Ibid., pp. 68–75.

67 Luna, Rafael. "Informal Annexations." *Intar Journal*, vol. 10, 2019, pp. 6–13.

68 "Seoul – 2.3 Population Changes in Hanseong." *Seoul – 2.3 Population Changes in Hanseong – CefiaWiki*, 19 Jan. 2017, http://cefia.aks.ac.kr:84/ index.php?title=Seoul_-_2.3_Population_Changes_in_Hanseong.

69 Ibid.

70 No, Chung-guk. *Seoul: A Journey Through 2000 Years of History*. Seoul: The City History Compilation Committee of Seoul, 2009, p. 250.

71 Ibid., p. 251.

72 Ibid.

73 Kim, Jae-Eun. "Gojong, a Misfortunate Monarch." *Korean Heritage*, vol. 42, 2018, pp. 8–15, p. 10.

74 No, Chung-guk. *Seoul: A Journey Through 2000 Years of History*. Seoul: The City History Compilation Committee of Seoul, 2009, p. 252.

75 Huh, Donghyun, and Vladimir Tikhonov. "The Korean Courtiers' Observation Mission's Views on Meiji Japan and Projects of Modern State Building." *Korean Studies*, vol. 29, no. 1, 2005, pp. 30–54, https://doi. org/10.1353/ks.2006.0004.

76 Ibid.

77 Kim, Sungbae. *Korea's Confucian Strategies Toward China During the Qing Dynasty and Their Implications*. Seoul: The East Asia Institute, 2013.

78 Kim, Jae-Eun. "Gojong, a Misfortunate Monarch." *Korean Heritage*, vol. 42, 2018, pp. 8–15, p. 10.

79 Song, Kue-jin. "Transformation of the Dualistic International Order into the Modern Treaty System in the Sino-Korean Relationship." *International Journal of Korean History*, vol. 15, no. 2, Aug. 2010, pp. 97–126.

80 No, Chung-guk. *Seoul: A Journey Through 2000 Years of History*. Seoul: The City History Compilation Committee of Seoul, 2009, p. 260.

81 Kang, Hong-bin, editor. *Seoul Museum of History: Places and Memories*. Seoul: Seoul Museum of History, 2013, p. 130.

82 No, Chung-guk. *Seoul: A Journey Through 2000 Years of History*. Seoul: The City History Compilation Committee of Seoul, 2009, p. 262.

83 Ibid., p. 265.

84 Ibid.

85 Kang, Hong-bin, editor. *Seoul Museum of History: Places and Memories*. Seoul: Seoul Museum of History, 2013, p. 112.

86 No, Chung-guk. *Seoul: A Journey Through 2000 Years of History*. Seoul: The City History Compilation Committee of Seoul, 2009, p. 265.

87 Simbirtseva, Tatiana, and Svetlana Levoshko. *Russian Architect Afanasy Seredin-Sabatin (1860–1921) in Korea: At the Roots of Modernity*. St. Petersburg: Institute of Theory of Architecture and Urban Planning, 2017, pp. 1–13.

88 "History of KEPCO." *Kepco*, https://home.kepco.co.kr/kepco/EN/A/ htmlView/ENAAHP002.do?menuCd=EN010102.

89 No, Chung-guk. *Seoul: A Journey Through 2000 Years of History*. Seoul: The City History Compilation Committee of Seoul, 2009, p. 277.

90 Hwang, Kyung Moon. "State Making Under Imperialism: Fragmentation and Consolidation in the Central State." *Rationalizing Korea the Rise of the Modern State, 1894–1945*. Oakland, CA: University of California Press, 2016, pp. 25–51, p. 33.

91 Ibid., pp. 25–51.

92 Ibid., p. 33.

93 Ibid., p. 34.

94 Henry, Todd A. *Assimilating Seoul: Japanese Rule and the Politics of Public Space in Colonial Korea, 1910–1945*. Berkeley: University of California Press, 2016, p. 29.

95 Park, Moonho. *The Understanding Korea Series (UKS) 4 Seoul*. Edited by The Center for International Affairs. Seongnam: The Academy of Korean Studies Press, 2015, p. 36.

96 Henry, Todd A. *Assimilating Seoul: Japanese Rule and the Politics of Public Space in Colonial Korea, 1910–1945*. Berkeley: University of California Press, 2016, p. 29.

97 Ibid.

98 Ibid.

99 Ibid.

100 Park, Young-Sin. "The Choson Industrial Exposition of 1915." *Binghamton University State University of New York*. Ann Arbor, MI: ProQuest LLC, 2019, pp. 1–461, p. 118.

101 "Terauchi ch'ongdog ŭi hunsi" [Instruction of Terauchi, the Government-General], *Maeil sinbo*, Apr. 14, 1914. Ibid. P. 103

102 No, Chung-guk. *Seoul: A Journey Through 2000 Years of History*. Seoul: The City History Compilation Committee of Seoul, 2009, p. 314.

103 Park, Moonho. *The Understanding Korea Series (UKS) 4 Seoul*. Edited by The Center for International Affairs. Seongnam: The Academy of Korean Studies Press, 2015, p. 38.

104 "Bank of Korea Money Museum, National Historic Site No. 280." *Bank of Korea*, 한국은행, www.bok.or.kr/eng/main/contents.do?menuNo=400265.

105 Kim, Kwang-jung. *Seoul, Twentieth Century, Growth and Change of the Last 100 Years*. Seoul: Seoul Development Institute, 2003, pp. 42–43.

106 Henry, Todd A. *Assimilating Seoul: Japanese Rule and the Politics of Public Space in Colonial Korea, 1910–1945*. Berkeley: University of California Press, 2016, p. 34.

107 This was calculated by digitalizing the map in Rhino 3D and comparing the area of the *iconic form blocks* to the total built area.

108 Jeon, Wu-Yong. *The Seoul City Wall: Walking the History of Seoul*. Seoul: The Seoul Institute, 2018, p. 113.

109 Henry, Todd A. *Assimilating Seoul: Japanese Rule and the Politics of Public Space in Colonial KOREA, 1910–1945*. Berkeley: University of California Press, 2016, p. 30.

110 Park, Moonho. *The Understanding Korea Series (UKS) 4 Seoul*. Edited by The Center for International Affairs. Seongnam: The Academy of Korean Studies Press, 2015, p. 42.

111 Henry, Todd A. *Assimilating Seoul: Japanese Rule and the Politics of Public Space in Colonial KOREA, 1910–1945*. Berkeley: University of California Press, 2016, p. 2.

112 Kim, Kwang-jung. *Seoul, Twentieth Century, Growth and Change of the Last 100 Years*. Seoul: Seoul Development Institute, 2003, pp. 444–450.

113 Henry, Todd A. *Assimilating Seoul: Japanese Rule and the Politics of Public Space in Colonial KOREA, 1910–1945*. Berkeley: University of California Press, 2016, p. 32.

114 Ibid., p. 37.

115 "Seoul – 4.1 Population Growth and Expansion of the Urban Center." *Seoul – 4.1 Population Growth and Expansion of the Urban Center – CefiaWiki*, 19 Jan. 2017, http://cefia.aks.ac.kr:84/index.php?title=Seoul_-_4.1_Population_Growth_and_Expansion_of_the_Urban_Center.

116 Lee, Hyang A. "Tracing Seoul's Modernity: The History of Urban Planning in Colonial Seoul." *Cross-Currents: East Asian History and Culture Review*, no. 27, June 2018, pp. 208–214.

117 Ibid.

118 Jung, Inha. *Architecture and Urbanism in Modern Korea*. Honolulu: University of Hawaii Press, 2014, p. 29.

119 "Seoul – 4.1 Population Growth and Expansion of the Urban Center." *Seoul – 4.1 Population Growth and Expansion of the Urban Center – CefiaWiki*, 19 Jan. 2017, http://cefia.aks.ac.kr:84/index.php?title=Seoul_-_4.1_Population_Growth_and_Expansion_of_the_Urban_Center.

120 "Urbanization Planning of Seoul." 서울정책아카이브 *Seoul Solution*, 30 Aug. 2021, www.seoulsolution.kr/en/node/2375.

121 Graham, Edward Montgomery. "The Miracle with a Dark Side: Korean Economic Development Under Park Chung Hee." *Reforming Korea's Industrial Conglomerates*. Washington, DC: Inst. for International Economics, 2005, pp. 11–50.

122 Graham, Edward Montgomery. "The Miracle with a Dark Side: Korean Economic Development Under Park Chung Hee." *Reforming Korea's Industrial Conglomerates*. Washington, DC: Inst. for International Economics, 2005, pp. 11–50.

123 Ibid., p. 16.

124 Kim, Joochul, and Sang-Chuel Choe. *Seoul: The Making of a Metropolis*. Chichester: Wiley, 1997.

125 Seoul Solution. "Urbanization Planning of Seoul." 서울정책아카이브 *Seoul Solution*, 30 Aug. 2021, https://seoulsolution.kr/en/node/2375.

126 Kim, Joochul, and Ch'oe Sang-ch'ŏl. *Seoul: The Making of a Metropolis*. Chichester: Wiley, 1997, p. 73.

127 Seoul Solution. "Urbanization Planning of Seoul." 서울정책아카이브 *Seoul Solution*, 30 Aug. 2021, https://seoulsolution.kr/en/node/2375.

128 "Seoul – 4.1 Population Growth and Expansion of the Urban Center." *Seoul – 4.1 Population Growth and Expansion of the Urban Center – CefiaWiki*, 19 Jan. 2017, http://cefia.aks.ac.kr:84/index.php?title=Seoul_-_4.1_Population_Growth_and_Expansion_of_the_Urban_Center.

129 Kim, Sun-Wung. "The Land Readjustment Program." 서울정책아카이브 *Seoul Solution*, Seoul: The Seoul Institute, 26 Apr. 2017, https://seoulsolution.kr/en/node/3446.

130 Ibid.

131 Ibid.

132 Ibid.

133 "Korea Land & Housing Corporation." *Lh.or.kr*, Korea Land and Housing Corporation, www.lh.or.kr/eng/contents/cont.do.

134 Kim, Joochul, and Sang-Chuel Choe. *Seoul: The Making of a Metropolis*. Chichester: Wiley, 1997, p. 107.

135 The Seoul Institute, Urban Planning, and Sun-Wung Kim. *Urban Planning & Management*. Seoul: Seoul Metropolitan Government, 2017, pp. 1–20.

136 Ibid.

137 Seoul Solution. "Management Policies for Seoul City Center & Changes." 서울정책아카이브 *Seoul Solution*, 10 Feb. 2017, https://seoulsolution.kr/en/content/management-policies-seoul-city-center-changes.

138 The Seoul Institute, Urban Planning, and Hyeon-Seok Min. *Sewun Mall Development Plan*. Seoul: Seoul Metropolitan Government, 2017, pp. 1–11.

139 Ibid.

140 http://english.seoul.go.kr/get-to-know-us/mayors-office/former-mayors/.

141 The Seoul Institute, Urban Planning, and Hyeon-Seok Min. *Sewun Mall Development Plan*. Seoul: Seoul Metropolitan Government, 2017, pp. 1–11.

142 Frampton, Kenneth. "The Generic Street as a Continuous Built Form." *On Streets*, edited by Stanford Anderson. Cambridge, MA: MIT Press, 1986, pp. 308–337.

143 "Seoul – 4.1 Population Growth and Expansion of the Urban Center." *Seoul – 4.1 Population Growth and Expansion of the Urban Center – CefiaWiki*, 19 Jan. 2017, http://cefia.aks.ac.kr:84/index.php?title=Seoul_-_4.1_Population_Growth_and_Expansion_of_the_Urban_Center.

144 Jung, Inha. *Architecture and Urbanism in Modern Korea*. Honolulu: University of Hawaii Press, 2014, p. 55.

145 Ibid., pp. 51–61.

146 Ibid., p. 50.

147 Ibid., p. 53.

148 Ibid.

149 Kim, Sun-Wung. "Urban Planning & Management." 서울정책아카이브 *Seoul Solution*, 31 Aug. 2017, www.seoulsolution.kr/en/node/3441.

150 Jung, Inha. *Architecture and Urbanism in Modern Korea*. Honolulu: University of Hawaii Press, 2014, p. 59.

151 Seoul Solution. "Urbanization Planning of Seoul." 서울정책아카이브 *Seoul Solution*, 30 Aug. 2021, https://seoulsolution.kr/en/node/2375.

152 The Seoul Institute, Urban Planning, and Sun-Wung Kim. *Urban Planning & Management*. Seoul: The Seoul Institute, 2017, pp. 1–20.

153 Patterson, Leanne, and Jae-Yong Jang, editors. *Seoul: A Journey Through 2000 Years of History*. Seoul: The City History Compilation Committee of Seoul, 2009.

154 Yang, Jae-Sub. "Seoul's Urban Redevelopment Policy." 서울정책아카이브 *Seoul Solution*, 10 Feb. 2017, https://seoulsolution.kr/en/content/seoul%E2%80%99s-urban-redevelopment-policy.

155 "Management Policies for Seoul City Center & Changes." 서울정책아카이브 *Seoul Solution*, 10 Feb. 2017, https://seoulsolution.kr/en/node/3442.

156 The Seoul Institute, Urban Planning, and Sun-Wung Kim. *Urban Planning & Management*. Seoul: The Seoul Institute, 2017, pp. 1–20.

157 Park, Jinhee, and John Hong. *Convergent Flux: Contemporary Architecture and Urbanism in Korea*. Basel: Birkhäuser, 2012, p. 34.

158 Jung, Inha. *Architecture and Urbanism in Modern Korea*. Honolulu: University of Hawaii Press, 2014, p. 105.

159 "About the World Trade Center Seoul: WTC Seoul." *About the World Trade Center Seoul | WTC Seoul*, www.wtcseoul.com/eng/introduce/intro02.do.

160 Ibid.

161 Fenton, Joseph. *Hybrid Buildings*. New York: Pamphlet Architecture, 1985, p. 8.

162 Ibid.

163 Koolhaas, Rem. "'Life in the Metropolis' or 'The Culture of Congestion'." *Architectural Design*, May 1977, pp. 319–325.

164 Ibid., p. 321.

165 Ibid., p. 322.

166 Ibid., p. 323.

167 Von Kempler, James. "Lotte World Tower: Seoul's First Supertall." *Council on Tall Buildings and Urban Habitat*, no. 1, 2018, pp. 12–19.

168 Ibid., p. 12.

169 Koolhaas, Rem, et al. *Small, Medium, Large, Extra-Large*. New York: Monacelli Press, 1998.

170 Easterling, Keller. *Extrastatecraft*. London: Verso, 2014.

171 *Chaebols* are large family-owned conglomerates.

172 Patterson, Leanne, and Jae-Yong Jang, editors. *Seoul: A Journey Through 2000 Years of History*. Seoul: The City History Compilation Committee of Seoul, 2009, p. 295.

173 Ibid.

174 "Lotte." *Lotte.co.kr*, www.lotte.co.kr/global/en/business/compDetail.do?compCd=L201.

175 *Hyundai Department Store Group History*, www.ehyundai.com/newPortal/group/GI/GI000002.do.

176 *Shinsegae Central City*, http://eng.shinsegaecentralcity.com/about#:~:text='Shinsegae%20Central%20City'%20is%20Korea's,Bus%20Terminal%20Co.%2C%20Ltd.

177 *Hyundai Department Store Group History*, www.ehyundai.com/newPortal/group/GI/GI000002.do.

178 Haksoon Yim. "Cultural Identity and Cultural Policy in South Korea." *The International Journal of Cultural Policy*, vol. 8, no. 1, 2002, pp. 37–48.

179 Yun, Jieheerah. *Globalizing Seoul: The City's Cultural and Urban Change*. London: Routledge, 2018.

180 Ibid., p. 4.
181 Park, Moonho. *The Understanding Korea Series (UKS) 4 Seoul.* Edited by The Center for International Affairs. Seoul: The Academy of Korean Studies Press, 2015, p. 159.
182 Maki, Fumihiko. *Investigations in Collective Form.* St. Louis: Washington University, 1964.
183 "Korea Land & Housing Corporation." *Lh.or.kr,* Korea Land and Housing Corporation, www.lh.or.kr/eng/contents/cont.do.
184 Woo-hyun, Shim. "GS E&C's XI Named Top Apartment Brand in Korea for 2nd Year." *The Korea Herald,* The Korea Herald, 8 Nov. 2017, www.koreaherald.com/view.php?ud=20171108000695.
185 Rem Koolhaas, *Madelon Vriesendorp. The City of the Captive Globe Project.* New York: Axonometric, 1972.
186 Kipnis, Jeffrey. "Jeffrey Kipnis – in Praise of Sloth, Indolence and All Other Forms of Torpor." *YouTube,* Architectural Association, 9 Oct. 2015, https://youtu.be/sEWLRDdD-dA.
187 It must be noted that the methodology of the Potato Plan is not copied here, only the graphic convention of abstracting groupings to describe the urban typological islands. As explained in a preceding chapter, Abercrombie's methodology focused on grouping social and industrial conditions, not architectural typologies. Yet, graphically, it provides for a quick reading of the city.

4 The Infra-Architectural Typology

During the decade of the 1960s, the possibilities of new urban growth inspired architects to envision structures that would organize entire cities as a built form. Primarily, avant-garde architecture by groups such as Team X, the Structuralist, the Situationist, and the Metabolist envisioned large-scale infra-architectural hybrids that resulted in projects for megastructures that would go mostly unrealized. The core principles these projects shared were the need for an infrastructural common as a new urban framework, the formation of new pedestrian grounds, and a better understanding of the permanent framework versus the temporary plug-ins. The target for these projects was to tackle urban sprawl and city form, which begs to question if these are considerable ideas for today's era of formless sprawling conurbations and megacities. For the city of Seoul, the concept of megastructures parallels the growing underground network in Seoul. This continuous megastructure organizes Seoul's composition of typological islands that exist aboveground as autonomous enclaves (the typological blocks), while offering an experiential layer of the city underground with architectural spatial qualities, programs, and urban appropriations. Arguably, this is a hybrid between infrastructure and architecture – infra-architecture (literal underground architecture).

In order to understand the underground of Seoul as a megastructure, it is important to review the catalytic factors that allowed the system to morph from a pure infrastructural transportation system to an architectural artifact. This hybridization process was led by metro-centric policies, financial models required for its development, and agendas for a cultural capital and a sharing economy that sought to optimize the existing infrastructure. These three factors allowed for the underground to become new pedestrian grounds with alternative programming and a formal linear urban growth system with the possibility of metabolic changes through plug-in units (urban blocks).

The existing state of the underground is comparable to the 1960s avant-garde proposals such as the Smithsons' Golden Lane, Constant's New Babylon, Maki's proposal for Mecca, the Freie Universität Berlin, and the proposal for Frankfurt Römerberg by Candilis, Josic, and Woods as their characteristics are present in Seoul's urban structure.

DOI: 10.4324/9781032684963-4

Description and Brief History of Seoul's Underground System

The underground network of Seoul is highly organized around the subway transportation system, yet it also comprises 3,253 civil defense shelters, pedestrian underpasses with 2,773 stores in 29 arcades, and almost 1,200 stores within the subway stations alone.[1] This underground environment grew in parallel to the rapid construction of the housing market, land appropriation, and urban planning as a bundled system mitigating the experience between the city's architectural typological islands aboveground while processing almost three billion rides for commuters annually below ground as indicated and updated daily from the national statistic of the Seoul Metro and KORAIL.[2] The system has its roots from the early tram lines established during the Daehan Empire and expanded during the Japanese occupation.[3] These were centered around the Central Business District, where the first electrical lines were laid out, and Seoul had a population of about 200,000 people.[4] With the Japanese urban expansion, the population grew to 900,000 by 1945 and quickly exceeded 1.5 million after the Korean War. A bus network was implemented to accommodate the population growth as the trams were discontinued by 1968 due to the increase in personal vehicles.[5] The increasing congestion between buses and vehicles required an additional solution that would ease the road traffic. Already in 1961, the Korean National Railroad had reviewed an underground subway connection between Seoul Station and Cheongnyangni Station within the First Five Year Economic Plan, later reviewed in the 10 year plan from 1965.[6] In 1970, President Park Chung Hee issued a directive for Seoul to develop mass transit, making the congestion of Seoul a national agenda. The first proposal for a subway network was designed around five radiating routes around a single nucleus, the CBD, which roughly followed the 1965 plan of Seoul. Quickly after in 1971, the construction of Line 1 began. Inaugurated on the 15th of August of 1974, Line 1 connected a 7.8 km span between Seoul Station and Cheongnyangni Station.[7] After the review of the 1965 plan of Seoul in 1970, the 1970 Modification of the "Basic Urban Plan" and the 1972 "Revised Comprehensive Plan," a polinuclear city was envisioned shaping the design for Line 2 as a circular line that connects the subcenters of Seoul (Yeongdeungpo and Gangnam). Construction started in 1978, and operations on May 22, 1984, completing a loop of 54.2 km.[8] Line 3 and 4 bisected the circular line mainly running on a north-south axis. These two were designed as connectors for Line 1 and 2 in order to increase their use. Line 3 and 4 opened on October 18, 1985.[9] The construction of Line 1 to 4 would be considered Phase 1 out of three phases that constitute the contemporary subway network.

Upon the completion of Phase 1, the population of Seoul had reached 9,646,000[10] and the subway ridership had increased by 10–16% year over year, maxing out its capacity by the end of the decade.[11] In order to alleviate the over saturation of the system, five new lines were proposed in 1988 by the city of Seoul, which required the backing of the central government, and focused on connecting further Line 1 and 2. In 1989, the Korea Research Institute for Human Settlements proposed a different plan, Phase 2, which would focus instead on the areas of Seoul that were still underserved by Phase 1. Each of the lines would have a specific focus. Line 5 would serve almost as a parallel line to Line 1, connecting east and west to the center of the city. The construction would be spread in several stages. A 14.5-km section from Wangsimni to Sangil-dong would open on November 15, 1995; 8.8 km from Baghwa to Kkachisan opened on March 20, 1996; 6.9 km from Macheon to Gangdong opened on March 30, 1996; 7.8 km from Yeouido to Kkachisan opened on August 12, 1996; 14.1 km from Yeouido to Wang-simni opened on December 30, 1996 completing the entire Line 5.[12] Line 6 would focus on underserved areas of Gangbuk only, such as Mapo-gu, south of Namsan, and the northeastern areas. Line 6 opened its first section on August 7, 2000, consisting of 6 stations in 4.2 km from Bonghwasan Mountain to Sangwolgok. The second section covered 30.9 km from Eungam to Sangwolgok and opened on December 15, 2000 except for four stations that opened later on March 9, 2001.[13] Line 7 would focus on alleviating the congestion of Gangnam, which was mainly serviced by Line 2, and partially by Line 3. Line 7 would first open a 19 km section from Jangam to Konkuk University on October 11, 1996; from Onsu to Sinpung on February 29, 2000; and from Sinpung to Konkuk University on August 1, 2000 to complete the entire line.[14] Line 8 would focus on the east side of Seoul, connecting Jamsil to the satellite city of Seongnam, which was developed for the displaced households from the 1970s. This would be completed in two sections; 13.1 km from Jamsil to Moran completed on November 23, 1996, and 4.6 km from Jamsil to Amsa completed on July 2, 1999.[15] This completed phase 2 of the subway network.

As Phase 2 started construction, the city began planning a third phase with four more additional lines to connect the leftover underserved areas that phase 2 did not service. At the same time, the city aimed at increasing the subway ridership and decreasing vehicular congestion. While the design for Line 9 had started in 1997, the Asian Financial Crisis forced Korea to seek assistance from the IMF. This economic pressure forced Phase 3 to be reviewed and canceled line 10, 11, and 12. Line 9 would remain, opening in 2009,[16] and a new plan emerged to work with the existing lines by expanding them, and servicing the remaining areas with Light Rail Train lines that would connect to the legacy system.

Paradigm Shift Toward a Metro-Centric City

Through three construction and planning phases, Seoul was able to build a robust subway network within four decades. Although its construction history seems purely infrastructural, this network would evolve into an infra-architectural hybrid layer due to metro-centric policies, financial models required for its development, and agendas for a cultural capital and a sharing economy that sought to optimize the existing infrastructure. This will provide the foundation for demonstrating how the underground network works as an architectural megastructure.

The first factor (metro-centric policies) deals with optimizing the connectivity between the subway system and the urban fabric to switch from private vehicles to mass transit. This formed a system that organizes the city based on connectivity nodes from each train station to the different urban blocks. Early on, the system was sized for 10 car trains and 210 m platforms to accommodate the growing population and ridership with the primary aim of decongesting the streets. In 1974, both private vehicles and the metro accounted for 1% each of the total transport. By the time Phase 2 was being planned in 1991, private vehicles constituted 25% and the metro 21% of the total ridership.[17] The metro expansion was seen as a solution to combat the increasing vehicular congestion and would be required to reach the majority of Seoul. Phase 2 was modified for this very purpose, reaching the underserved areas from Phase 1. Phase 3 aimed to complete the outreach of underserved areas but was cut short after the cancellation of line 10, 11, and 12. By 2010, the use of private vehicles accounted for 24% of the total transportation share, despite the increase in subway ridership to 36%.[18] This meant that the number of vehicles was still increasing in parallel to the increase in subway ridership. In May of 2013, the Seoul Transport Vision 2030 was announced aiming to produce a paradigm shift from individual mobility through private vehicles to more collective, environmentally friendly, and sustainable modes that would largely rely on the subway.[19] As Joonho Ko[20] points out, the Seoul Metropolitan Government adopted the slogan "Liveable Seoul without relying on cars" as well as three key concepts: "human oriented transportation," "shared transportation," and "environmentally friendly transportation."[21] With this new vision, all residents should be able to reach a metro within a 10-minute walk, and the metro should be used as the primary form of transportation. The plan envisions a reduction of private vehicle ridership by 30% and an increase of green transport modes to 80% requiring an integration of intermodal systems, prioritizing the pedestrian over the car.[22] Ko's report for the city of Seoul regarding the 2030 vision shows a success for the case studies already realized by Sinchon station.

> A survey conducted after six months showed a 34% reduction in traffic accidents, an 11% increase in bus users, and a 4.2% increase in sales for shops in the local area. In addition, the proportion of citizens satisfied with the transit mall rose from 12% to 70%.[23]

One of the first tasks with this agenda was connecting the underserved areas to the subway system, which would be the backbone for the 2030

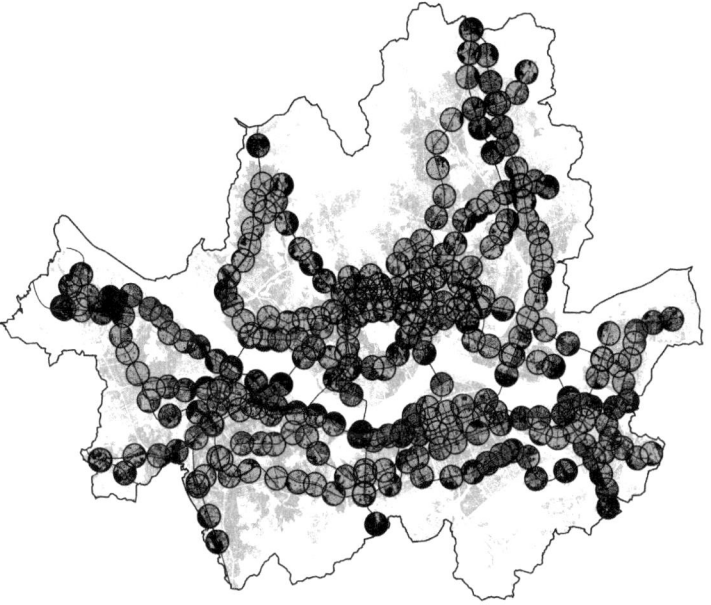

Figure 4.1 Subway coverage based on a 600 m walking radius from each station.

vision. Thirty-eight percent of Seoul was still considered to be poorly serviced at the time, yet due to the incurred debt from the subway construction, no further heavy traffic subway lines could be planned.[24] In 2014, master planning commenced for a Light Rapid Transit project which would focus on the remaining poorly serviced areas of Seoul using light rail services that could handle 10,000 passengers per kilometer per day and connect to the existing network.[25] The bus network would readjust their routes for any remaining underserved areas and focus on the connection to the subway stations.

The result of this planning is a city organized and formed through subway lines. Rather than trying to read Seoul as a sprawling conurbation, Seoul can be read through linear urban formations where growth or expansion follows the metro line and density is organized around its nodes. This produces a concentration of commercial activity around subway stations, which act as catalysts for each neighborhood. The 600-m walking radius from each subway exit serves as either a virtual and/or physical connection to the architectural typological islands aboveground. The density of amenities and services can be mapped independently to show the importance of each station as an urban node.

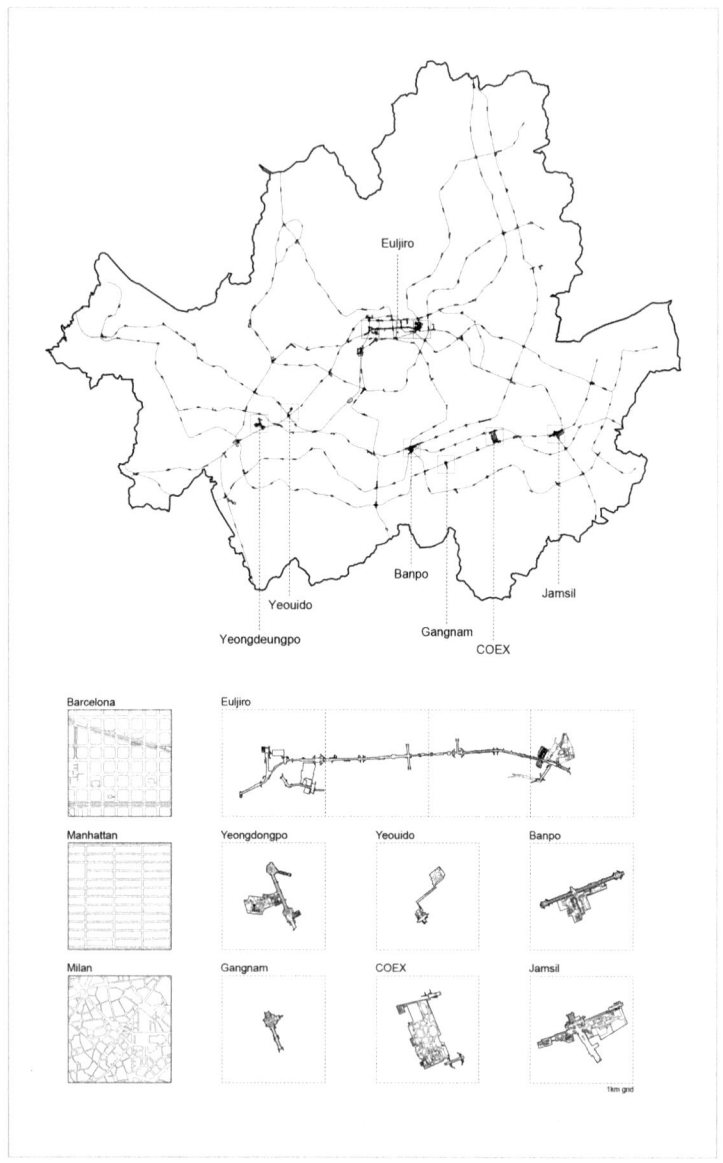

Figure 4.2 Subway lines and stations as horizontal skyscrapers.

Abstractly, the 600-m radii do not have to touch every building, instead they connect to the architectural typological islands aboveground as a whole. While the aim of the transport plan is to have no one walk more than 600 m to a station, for a pedestrian-friendly megacity to work, the island is what needs to connect to the station and not all the buildings within the island because of the urban scale. Perhaps in a smaller, tighter city, 600 m to every building from a station is achievable. For the Seoul megacity formation, each island in itself is already a walkable condition; superblocks are similar to the super-manzanas program in Barcelona,[26] for example. Each island also has a strong architectural identity, and micro mobility could perhaps be resolved within each block. Not having the whole typological island inside the radius is not a negative condition but an organized solution for mass transit linked to a large-scale urban formation.

The islands act as urban subunits that can be added and changed over time similar to the ideals of the Metabolist. When compared to the Metabolist megastructures though, the scale of plug-ins is different. In Maki's proposal for Mecca, for example, the megastructure was the infrastructure that organized temporary housing. Individual temporary houses were the units. The same is the case for the Tokyo Bay project. In the case of Seoul, the typological islands are the urban units that can change over time as needed per market demand, which is how the current urban mutations are happening. The generic urban fabric is turned into a typological island within walking distance of a subway station.

More concretely, the pedestrian-friendly agenda also had a physical tangible effect on the typology of stations that transformed them to architectural buildings with programs, and public spaces. The shift from the car to the pedestrian would allow for the already existing underground tunnels to become a means for mobilizing pedestrians across city blocks, separated from traffic. Underground bomb shelter remnants from the Korean War were transformed and connected as pedestrian passageways and shopping arcades linked to the subway system. Originally intended as shelter, most of these underground structures worked independently, yet, as the subway system grew as an integrated part of the shelter system, the passageways started connecting to the subway tunnels wherever the proximity allowed. Mapping all the underground stations from the nine subway lines, one sees a concentration of underground structures occurring primarily in the Central Business District and subscores where the density is the highest. These stations have morphed their form that is originally based on the linear and slender parameters of a 210 m platform to one that sustains larger facilities such as underground shopping centers.

The formal anatomy of the stations allows for extended concourses to fill with programs, mainly commercial, while connecting blocks with additional subway exits. This allows for longer trajectories to be perceived as pedestrian friendly or connected since the 10 minute walking radius from each exit has

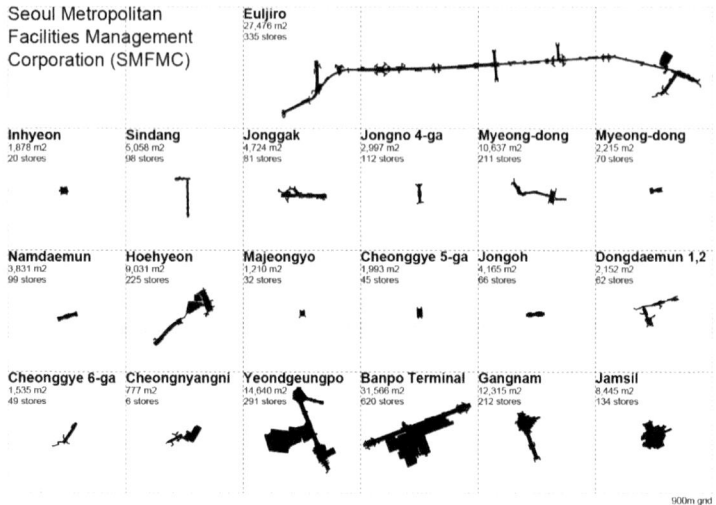

Figure 4.3 Underground shopping centers managed by the SMFMC.

an expanded reach rather than calculating a 600 m radius from the center of the station.

Programming the Megastructure

In a recorded lecture by Reyner Banham at the Architectural Association, he quotes what Denise Scott Brown considered to be the fatal idea for megastructures in the 1960s. "What is being omitted is a view of the city as a set of interrelated activities. There must still be physical relationships, economic, social, political, otherwise, what is everybody doing up there together with everybody else in those megastructures."[27]

While the first factor for understanding the underground network of Seoul as an architectural megastructure has to do with its connective nature, this quote by Denise Scott Brown raises the key factor for the criticism megastructures received when first proposed. For the underground network of Seoul to work as an architectural layer of the city, it must also offer an alternative mode of operation rather than purely infrastructure for mobility. For Seoul, alternative urban programming was achieved through the financial models required for the development of the underground, and more recent agendas for a cultural capital and a sharing economy that sought to optimize the existing infrastructure at the beginning of the 21st century.

During Park Chung Hee's leadership in the 1960s, the central government commenced the planning of the metro while meeting regularly with Japan to secure technical cooperation and financing through loans.[28] These loans would be used in Phase 1 mainly for the construction of Line 1 and 2, while depleting the financing for Line 3 and 4. As no further loans could be obtained from Japan, the government sought alternative financing, and the city studied foreign models of financing through private capital. Under the approval of the central government, the Seoul Subway Construction Headquarter was established in 1970 by the private sector for this portion of the construction, but due to its poor performance, it was disbanded in 1981, and replaced by the Seoul Metro Subway Corporation.[29] Upon the completion of Line 3 and 4 in 1985, the subway construction had amounted to an unmanageable debt of over 2 trillion KRW due to this phase relying heavily on high loan ratios.[30] The debt ratio for Line 1 was 55%, Line 2 was 63%, and Line 3 and 4 was 87%. Learning from Phase 1, Phase 2 had further central government involvement in order to reduce the debt ratio.[31]

The Asian Financial Crisis which required the central government to borrow from the IMF dampened the financing for Phase 3, canceling line 10, 11, and 12.[32] As the only remaining line for Phase 3, Line 9 would be financed through a public–private partnership consisting of a consortium of foreign and domestic companies. Following a Buy-Transfer-Operate (BTO) model, a private operator would be allowed to run Line 9 for 30 years before returning operations to the Seoul Metropolitan Government.[33] This would reduce the financial burden on the city of Seoul. As an incentive for the private sector, the Seoul Metropolitan Government would negotiate a minimum revenue guarantee (MRG) in the case there was a discrepancy between projected revenue from fares, and the actual revenue once in operation.[34] For the first five years, the government guaranteed 90% of the discrepancy, 80% for the second five years, and 70% for the third five years. The private operator would also be allowed to decide on the price for the fare. This model favored the private operator, and the price hikes would eventually cause a problem.

While the financing for construction relied on loans by the central government, foreign capital, and private equity, the repayments on the loans would have to come from the revenue of fares due to the MRG model. In 2005, the MRG was switched to a minimum cost compensation (MCC) model instead.[35] Rather than depending on the fare, the subsidies would now depend on the total revenue generated by the system. This would take into account the rental spaces that were incorporated into each station for commercial use as an additional source of operating income. Not accounting for the underground shopping centers, there are 1,192 stores operating in the 728 stations.[36] While the percentage of rental income (5%) is much less than the fare income (95%),[37] having these spaces has allowed the city to extend as an underground layer by providing a diversity of programs beyond just retail. Stations offer a variety

Figure 4.4 Collage of underground activities and programs.

Figure 4.4 (Continued)

of programs including spaces for production, work, culture, social amenities, food, and retail, some targeting programs for the neighboring communities.[38]

Because the stations are nodes of congregation for commuting around the city, the 10-minute radius around each station presents an increased number of services and amenities asserting a connection to the neighboring blocks. This connection presents the possibility for subway stations to become tools for promoting cultural industries while optimizing the use of infrastructural spaces. Gyeongbokgung station on Line 3, for example, sits at the corner of Gyeongbokgung, the main palace of the Joseon Dynasty and one of the main tourist destinations in Seoul. The station uses a section of its concourse as the Seoul Metro Museum in order to extend the experience while guaranteeing a larger exposure to a smaller attraction.[39]

While the previous example sits below a major tourist attraction (Gyeongbokgung palace), the concept of using the subway stations as cultural spaces that represent the blocks aboveground can also be a reflection of the "Cultural Capital" program, optimizing the use of existing infrastructure in other areas of Seoul for the purpose of promoting cultural industries. Semi-industrial areas around Seoul have been transforming in the past decade as integral gentrification zones, where industry is maintained as a cultural attraction. This is promoted by the Seoul Metropolitan Government, which has spent over 300 billion won to enhance smart city, and smart economies ecosystems.[40] Seongsu, for example, known for its shoe industry has transformed the area around the station as a shoe street that showcases handmade shoes. Euljiro, known for its electronics and fabricators, is also seeking ways to develop the area without displacing its industry. Seongsu Station and Euljiro 3 station, both on the green line, have transformed their stations as cultural connectors by introducing exhibition spaces within the stations that present the history of each respective area. Most people traveling to these areas by subway, would encounter these exhibitions as the entry points to the neighborhoods. The success of these subway stations as cultural neighborhood venues has expanded throughout Seoul and included as part of the tourist attractions such as the Noksapyeong Station Underground Art Garden, Seoul Hall of Urbanism and Architecture, Metro Farm in Dongjak Station, and Jonggak Station Solar Garden.[41]

> Today, the metro is more than a simple mode of transport, it has increasingly become a basis for economic and cultural activity. This trend could be helpful in taking aggressive steps to develop the stations and utilize the surrounding land to secure new sources of income.[42]

System as a Megastructure

Ever since the conception of the underground system in Seoul, the importance of the stations as activity nodes due to their connection to transport has produced an incentive for the environments aboveground to connect to the underground. This has allowed for the system to keep on expanding horizontally underground, connecting the different islands aboveground. The Central Business District underground network demonstrates this condition by linking five stations along Line 2 through one continuous 3.3-km passage under Euljiro. As new buildings develop along Euljiro, their basement levels connect to the underground passage extending their programs to the public space regardless if they are public buildings or private buildings as there is a reciprocity of benefits. Private buildings get a larger exposure to consumers, while public buildings get greater numbers of visitors by connecting to the system. This reciprocity generates a diversity of environments that answers the incertitude the original megastructures faced on their usability and connectivity. Much of the criticism megastructures received in the 1960s had to do with their connectivity to transport, density, and programming, as noted by Kenneth Frampton.[43] Projects like Golden Lane offered a pedestrian deck that connected housing blocks, yet they were transitory spaces, vector spaces of flow rather than programmed spaces with any use.

While the Euljiro underground offers a diversity of retail spaces, it continues to expand through a series of interventions that aim at transforming the underground as a cultural destination rather than just a transitory consumer space. This transformation has been executed gradually through city initiatives and public competitions. In 2015, the Seoul Metropolitan Government announced the Sejong-daero Historic Cultural Space Design Competition for "creating a space for integration of existing historic cultural heritages and contemporary urban space."[44] Completed in December of 2018, this has become the Seoul Hall of Urbanism and Architecture, a museum and exhibition space directly linked to the subway network through exit 4 of Line 1. The majority of the program exists underground in three basement levels. Its location, right across the street from City Hall, forms a cultural extension of the renovated Citizens Hall, a support space for the citizens of Seoul located in the basement of City Hall.

In 2016, the city of Seoul unveiled a plan to expand the underground by connecting from City Hall to Gwanghwamun Station, and from the Sejong Center for the Performing Arts to Jonggak Station.[45] The system would expand to 4.4 km, connecting 12 subway stations. This expansion would begin to connect underground passageways across lines (Line 2 and Line 5), starting to form an underground grid coordinated between the public and private sector. Its construction was programmed to take place between 2020 and 2025.

On October 12, 2018, an international design competition was announced for the redevelopment of Gwanghwamun Square, one of the most symbolic spaces of Seoul. The plaza currently marks the north-south axis extending from Gyeongbokgung to Jongno-ro and sits as a median between 12 traffic lanes (6 on each side). This competition reclaims the space as a historic symbolic plaza and connects the surrounding blocks in an area of 126,100 m².

The winning entry by CA Design proposed to unmask all the historic layers through a dual plaza – aboveground and underground. The underground extends Gwanghwamun Station as a 400 m underground plaza.[46] "The underground square will be a space of relaxation, culture, education, and experience, filled with year-round cultural events such as concerts and exhibitions."[47]

In May of 2020, the New Jongno-gu Government Complex Design Competition was announced.[48] While the main focus of this competition was to design the new district office, it also integrated social and cultural facilities, and expanded the underground connection to Gwanghwamun Station. This massive office complex of 66,000 m² forms part also of the redevelopment intent for the area to become more pedestrian friendly and active at all times of the day, and hence the connection to the underground and diversity in public programming are of extreme importance.

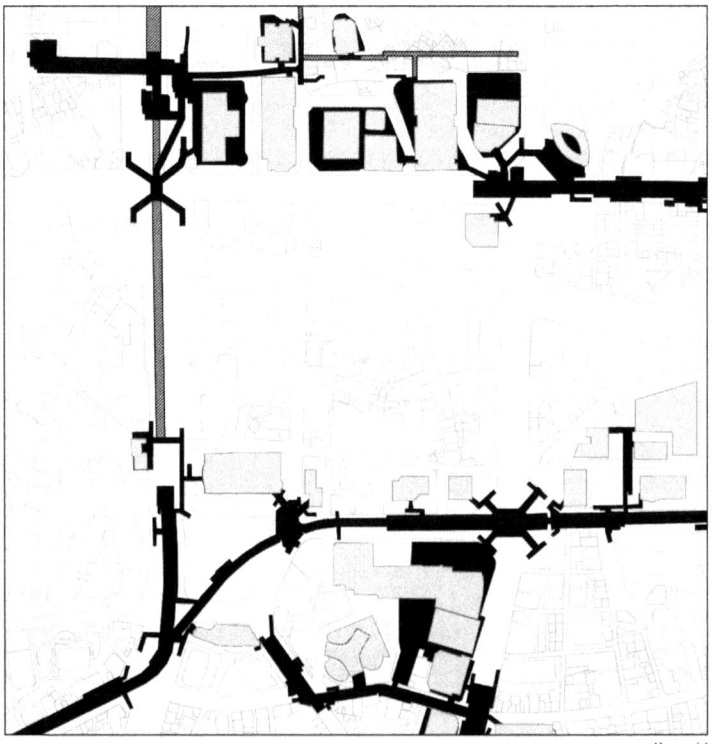

1km grid

Figure 4.5 Jongno underground network as a megastructure that connects different buildings and programs.

Through all of these interventions, the underground system has expanded its scope of use to include cultural, civic, production, educational, entertainment, and retail facilities in parallel to servicing mass-transit and pedestrian accessibility. It has evolved into an active layer of the city allowing for a varied programming as well as urban appropriations, and events. Mapping the Central Business District Underground shows a connective spine formation to which buildings can plug into. This resembles the ideals of the Metabolism and Structuralist, which allow for organic growth while maintaining a permanent organizational composition.

The scale at which the Euljiro network has expanded is comparable to the scale of the visionary proposals from the 1960s, showing that it is possible to build such a structure. When comparing the span of the Euljiro Underground network to Constant's New Babylon in Paris and Amsterdam or the Smithson Golden Lane in London, the Euljiro structure covers entire sections of city cores achieving the pedestrian connection between buildings and blocks that was desired by the 1960s proposals. Constant's Situationist vision for such a structure over Amsterdam or Paris seemed to have avoided the historic centers as his megastructures would span aboveground in a highly disruptive manner. The Euljiro model would render a different experience as it is underground, but perhaps it still achieves the "dérive" from the Situationist. One can enter the megastructure at one point, transit through the pedestrian passageways, and appear at a different point in the city, experiencing the city as different typological island environments in Seoul, bypassing generic urban fabric. This is comparable to the experience Guy Debord was mapping in "the Naked City" for Paris.

In comparison to the controversial LOMEX project for Lower Manhattan, the Euljiro Underground would cover from NOHO to Rockefeller Center through Broadway. Paul Rudolph's proposal was a brutalist hybrid, merging housing with the highway in order to hide the road infrastructure. It could be argued that when comparing Euljiro to LOMEX, Euljiro presents a case for such a megastructure to operate under this density in a non-intrusive manner. Both structures, Euljiro (built) and LOMEX (unbuilt), are almost identical in length, 3.3 km. Seoul has a density of 16,560 population per square kilometer,[49] while New York has a density of 10,750 population per square kilometer.[50] Both structures would run through financial cores of their respective city with very similar typologies primarily composed of tower blocks within the CBD in Seoul and Lower Manhattan in New York City. Hence, the Euljiro megastructure could be conceptualized as possible in Manhattan.

Although the largest extent for underground connections has focused mainly on the CBD, similar projects are occurring in other major subcenters, mainly Yeongdeungpo and Gangnam, through public and private partnerships. Yeongdeungpo has grown its underground through two private developments, Times Square Mall in 2009 and the International Financial Center in 2012. The Times Square Mall has fused its two underground shopping levels with

SEOUL OF ISLANDS
Psychogeographic Mapping

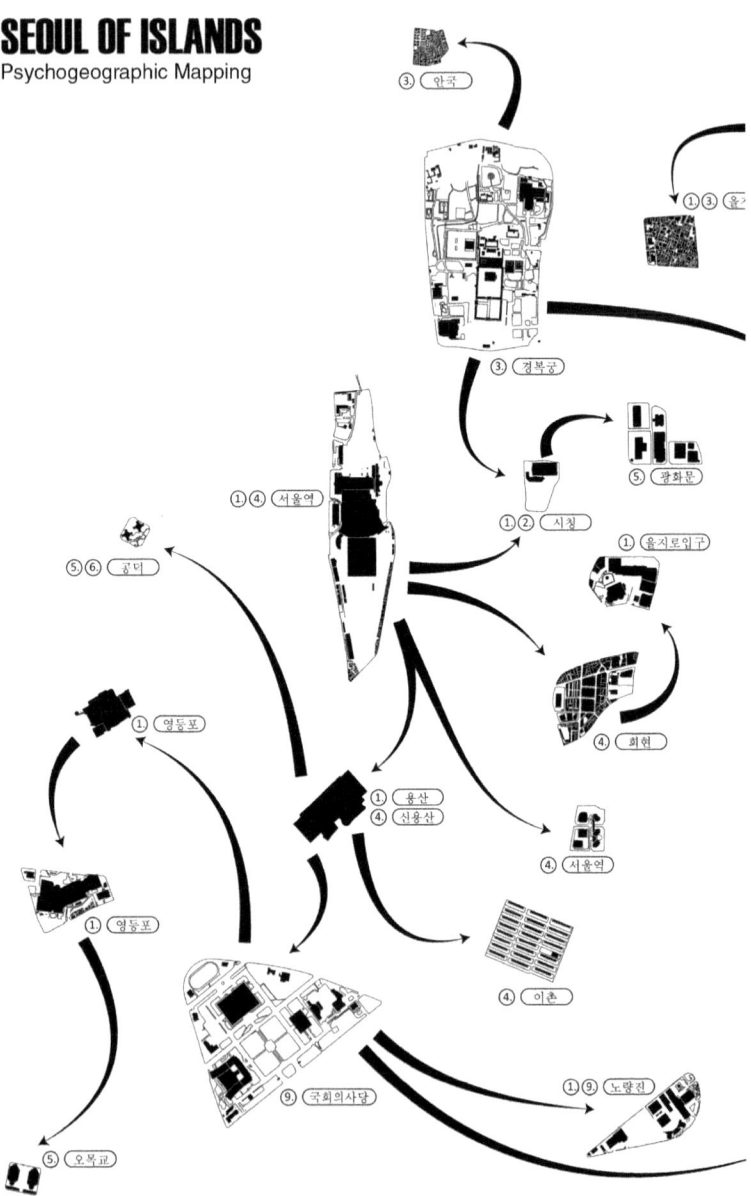

Figure 4.6 Psychogeographic map of Seoul.

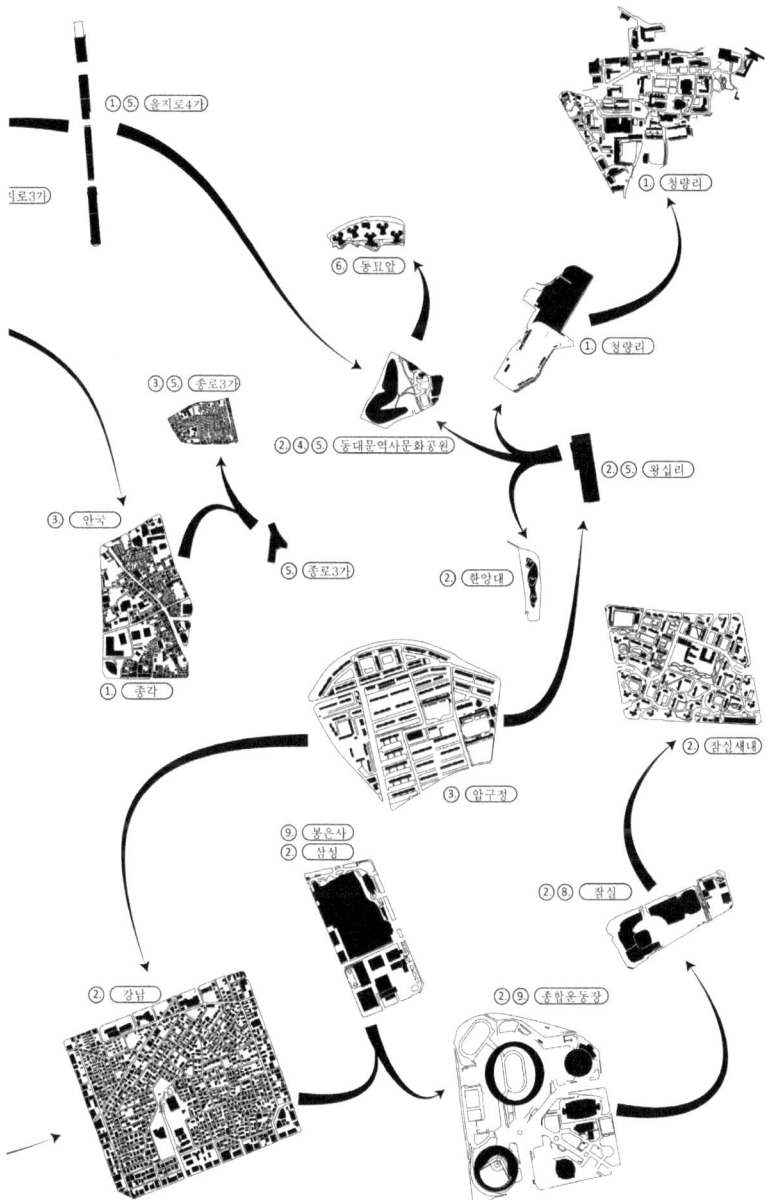

Figure 4.6 (Continued)

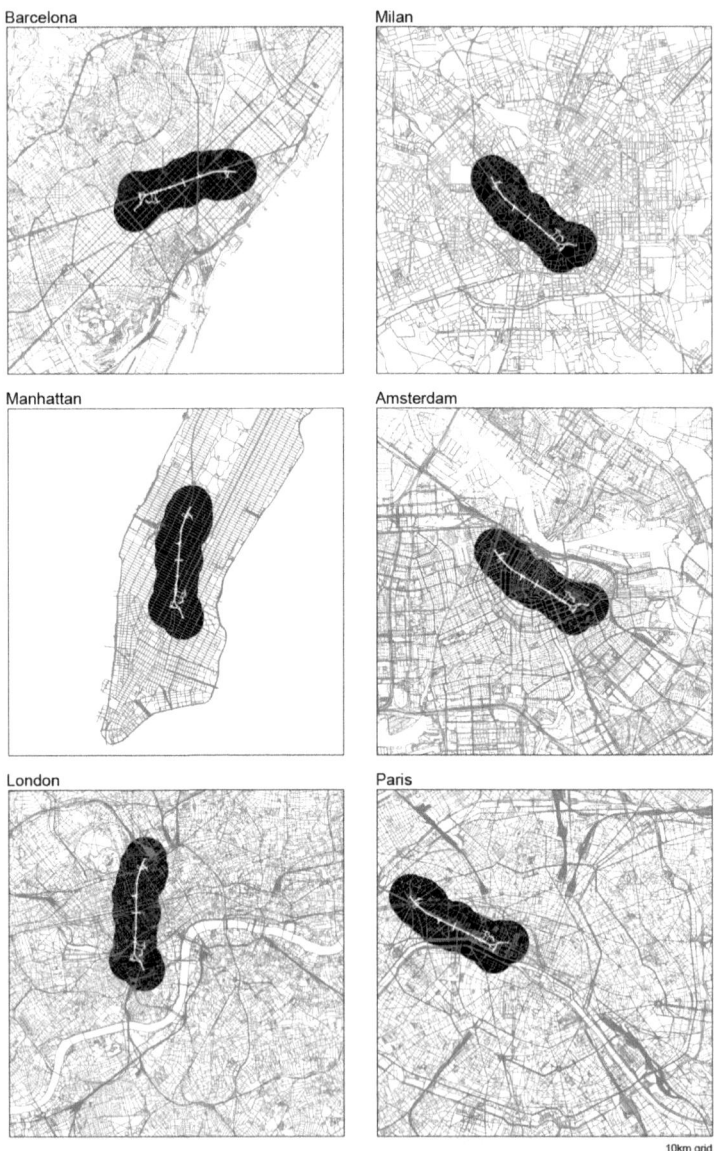

Figure 4.7 Euljiro underground overlayed on different Western cities to show the scale.

Lotte Department Store's underground and Yeongdeungpo Underground Shopping District covering a perimeter of roughly 84,000 m². The perimeter was calculated based on floor plans. The mall itself has "shopping and cultural facilities over a total of 300,000 square meters."[51] The IFC Mall covers a perimeter of almost 29,000 m² and is connected to Yeouido Station on Line 5 through a 230-m passage.[52]

Gangnam's largest underground networks are the Banpo Express Bus Terminal, Gangnam Station, COEX, and Jamsil Station. The Starfield/COEX Mall makes up the underground of the COEX complex connecting Samseong Station in Line 2 and Bongeunsa Station in Line 9. This covers an area approximately seven Manhattan blocks making it Asia's largest underground shopping mall.[53] At the same time, due to the infrastructure provided by COEX and the World Trade Center, this node has become an economic hub. In order to build up and support this effect, the Gangnam Intermodal Transit Center was proposed in 2017 to run under Yeongdong Daero next to the COEX Center as a way to upgrade an integral transportation infrastructure hub to the complex. The winning entry by Dominique Perrault, "Light Walk," would develop 160,000 m² of underground programming of which 72,000 m² would be for commercial use.[54] In parallel, the Hyundai Motor Group also proposed in 2016 the Global Business Center (GBC) to be built as a super tall skyscraper superseding the Lotte World Tower. The GBC will feature a sunken square that connects back to COEX through the Intermodal Transit Center.[55]

The incremental growth of the underground network in Seoul, both as an architectural space and as an infrastructural network, reveals a megastructure model for urbanization that performs the ideals that were once conceptualized by Team X, the Situationist, the Metabolist, and the Structuralist such as an infrastructural commons that formalizes as the guiding urban framework, production of new connective pedestrian grounds, and issues of organic growth. It must be reiterated that the key megastructural proposals such as the Smithsons' Golden Lane, Constant's New Babylon, Maki's Mecca, Candilis – Josic – Woods's Frankfurt Römerberg, and Rudolph's LOMEX were criticized by Denise Scott Brown for their programmatic use, by Kenneth Frampton for their lack of integration between circulation networks, and failure to provide a viable housing solution, and by Jane Jacobs for their disruptive nature in bisecting the city. More importantly, they never solidified as actual systems of urbanization, meaning, they never provided an expansive framework for urban growth. Instead, the few examples built show how megastructures eventually became urban islands that read more as megaform blocks as shown with the Seun Sangga case in Seoul. Perhaps the intended scale of execution was never achieved, and the proposals were out of context in terms of time and density of population, which may have led to their dismissal. The previously stated characteristics of the underground network of Seoul demonstrate that these ideas are existent and thriving under the contemporary dense conditions of Seoul. The network has provided new commons, a new pedestrian ground and connectivity among autonomous "plug-in" typological islands. The clear difference between Seoul and the avant-garde is the composition of air rights from the 1960s as opposed to the underground rights in Seoul. Perhaps by being underground as opposed to aboveground, there is still a predominant image of infrastructure over architecture in the underground. This is changing through the architectural interventions on the infrastructural space. Lastly, one positive effect of being underground is the ability for this network to expand and produce new nodes. This offers a model for a controlled urbanization that can be described as interior urbanism or infra-architectural urbanism connecting distinct experiences between underground and aboveground through an interior space.

Notes

1 "Underground Shopping Center: Global_main_en>Facility Management." *Underground Shopping Center | global_main_en>Facility Management*, Seoul Facilities Corporation, www.sisul.or.kr/global/main/en/sub/shoppingcenter.jsp.
2 서울교통공사. *서울교통공사*, www.seoulmetro.co.kr/kr/board.do?menuIdx=548. Korail. "KORAIL." *코레일*, info.korail.com/mbs/www/subview.jsp?id=www_020203010000.
3 Kang, Hong-bin, editor. *Seoul Museum of HISTORY: Places and Memories*. Seoul: Seoul Museum of History, 2013, p. 136, p. 184, p. 232.
4 "Seoul – 4.1 Population Growth and Expansion of the Urban Center." *Seoul – 4.1 Population Growth and Expansion of the Urban Center – CefiaWiki*, 19 Jan. 2017, http://cefia.aks.ac.kr:84/index.php?title=Seoul_-_4.1_Population_Growth_and_Expansion_of_the_Urban_Center.
5 Ko, Joonho. "A Guide to Transportation Policy (General)." *서울정책아카이브 Seoul Solution*, Seoul Institute, 10 Feb. 2017, www.seoulsolution.kr/en/content/guide-transportation-policy-general.
6 South Korea, The Seoul Institute, Metro Policy, and Seungjun Kim. *Construction of the Seoul Metro – The Driver Behind Sustainable Urban Growth & Change*. Seoul: The Seoul Institute, 2017, pp. 193–205, p. 195.
7 Ibid.
8 Ibid., p. 196.
9 Ibid.
10 "Seoul – 4.1 Population Growth and Expansion of the Urban Center." *Seoul – 4.1 Population Growth and Expansion of the Urban Center – CefiaWiki*, 19 Jan. 2017, http://cefia.aks.ac.kr:84/index.php?title=Seoul_-_4.1_Population_Growth_and_Expansion_of_the_Urban_Center.
11 South Korea, The Seoul Institute, Metro Policy, and Seungjun Kim. *Construction of the Seoul Metro – The Driver Behind Sustainable Urban Growth & Change*. Seoul: The Seoul Institute, 2017, pp. 193–205, p. 196.

12 Seoul Metro. "Intro to Seoul Metro: Overview and History." *Seoul Metro*, 2017, www.seoulmetro.co.kr/en/page.do?menuIdx=653.

13 Ibid.

14 Ibid.

15 Ibid.

16 Ibid.

17 Kim, Seungjun. "[Metro] a Driving Force for Sustainable Development and REMARKABLE Change, Seoul METROPOLITAN SUBWAY." 서울정책아카이브 *Seoul Solution*, City of Seoul, 10 Nov. 2016, seoulsolution.kr/en/node/1802.

18 Ibid.

19 "Seoul Transportation Vision 2030 –." *Official Website of The*, 5 Oct. 2016, english.seoul.go.kr/policy/traffic/seoul-transportation-vision-2030/.

20 Joonho Ko is the director of Megacity Research Center (MRC) in the Seoul Institute, the think tank of the Seoul Metropolitan Government, Korea.

21 Ko, Joonho. "Seoul Transport Vision 2030." *Urban Solutions*, no. 6, Feb. 2015, pp. 28–35.

22 Seoul Solution. "Vision 2030 for a PEDSTRIAN-FRIENDLY SEOUL." 서울정책아카이브 *Seoul Solution*, Seoul Solution, 18 Nov. 2016, seoulsolution.kr/en/node/1769.

23 Ko, Joonho. "Seoul Transport Vision 2030." *Urban Solutions*, no. 6, Feb. 2015, p. 33.

24 Kim, Seungjun, and Joonho Ko. *Seoul's Light-Rail Projects Driven by Private Investment for Poorly Serviced Areas*. Seoul: Seoul Institute, 2017, pp. 229–238.

25 Ibid.

26 "Superilles." *Bienvenido a Superilles | Superilles*, 2022, https://ajuntament.barcelona.cat/superilles/es/.

27 "Megastructures 1." Performance by Reyner Banham, *AA School*, Artnet, 15 Oct. 1974, www.aaschool.ac.uk/publicprogramme/whatson/megastructures-1.

28 South Korea, The Seoul Institute, Metro Policy, and Seungjun Kim. *Construction of the Seoul Metro – The Driver Behind Sustainable Urban Growth & Change*. Seoul: The Seoul Institute, 2017, pp. 193–205, p. 195.

29 Ibid., p. 196.

30 Ibid.

31 Ibid., p. 201.

32 Ibid., p. 197.

33 Transportation Metro Policy, et al. *Introduction of the Rapid Urban Railway System Construction of Subway Line 9*. Seoul: The Seoul Institute, 2017, pp. 1–8.

34 Ibid.

35 Ibid.

36 "Seoul Transportation Corporation Subway Shopping Malls." 서울열린데이터광장, *Seoul Transportation Corporation*, 3 June 2020, data.seoul.go.kr/dataList/OA-12927/F/1/datasetView.do.

37 Ibid.

38 Ibid.

39 *Seoul Metro Art Center*, Seoul Tourism Organization, 29 Apr. 2019, en-
   glish.visitseoul.net/attractions/Seoul-Metro-Art-Center-en_/29325.
40 "Creation of Industrial Ecosystem for Smart City." *Policy Tasks < Digital Seoul*, Seoul Metropolitan Government, 2021, digital.seoul.go.kr/eng/
   smart-seoul/policy-tasks/smart-economy.
41 "Seoul Guided Walking Tour." *Seoul Underground – A Different Plane
   of Time*, Seoul Tourism Organization, 27 Aug. 2020, english.visit-
   seoul.net/walking-tour/Seoul-Underground/34964?letterSn=1822<con
   tent=200908_Seoul+Underground%3Cbr%3EA+Different+Plane+of+
   Time.
42 Seungjun Kim. *Construction of the Seoul Metro – The Driver Behind Sustainable Urban Growth & Change*. Seoul: Seoul Institute, p. 204.
43 Kenneth Frampton. "The Generic Street as a Continuous Built Form." *On
   Streets*, edited by Stanford Anderson. Cambridge, MA: MIT Press, 1986,
   pp. 308–337.
44 Santos, Sabrina. "Open Call: Sejong-Daero Historic Cultural Space
   Design Competition." *ArchDaily*, ArchDaily, 11 Aug. 2015, www.
   archdaily.com/771508/open-call-sejong-daero-historic-cultural-space-
   design-competition.
45 Ssunha. "[Urban Planning News] Seoul Opens a 'New 31,000 ㎡ Underground City' from City Hall to Sejong-Daero." 서울정책아카이브 *Seoul
   Solution*, Seoul Metropolitan Government, 22 Nov. 2016, https://tinyurl.
   com/mrykhn4f.
46 Competition Organizing Committee, Gwanghwamun Square Project Group:
   "International Design Competition for New Gwanghwamun Square." 새로
   운 광화문광장 조성 설계공모, *Seoul Metropolitan Government*, 2018,
   https://project.seoul.go.kr/view/viewDetailArch.do?cpttMstSeq=229.
47 "Seoul's New Gwanghwamun to Return to the Citizens in 2021 with Announcement of International Design Competition Winners." *Urban Planning News*, Seoul Metropolitan Government, Jan. 2019, https://tinyurl.
   com/4kb3pb5v. Accessed 15 Apr. 2022.
48 New Office Construction Team at Jongno-gu Office. "The New Jongno-
   Gu Government Complex Design Competition." 종로구 통합청사 설계
   공모, Seoul Metropolitan Government, 2020, https://project.seoul.go.kr/
   view/viewDetailArch.do?cpttMstSeq=317.
49 "서울의 통계." 서울시 정보소통광장, Seoul Institute, 2021, opengov.
   seoul.go.kr/stat.
50 "Population – New York City Population." *Planning-Population-NYC
   Population Facts – DCP*, www1.nyc.gov/site/planning/planning-level/
   nyc-population/population-facts.page#:~:text=New%20York%20has%20
   the%20highest,27%2C000%20people%20per%20square%20mile.
51 KYUNGBANG CO, LTD. "Korea's No. 1 Shopping Complex Times
   Square." *TIMESSQUARE > about Us*, KYUNGBANG CO, LTD, 2022,
   www.timessquare.co.kr/?controller=eng&action=about.
52 The numbers were calculated based on floor plans by the author.
53 Seoul Tourism Organization. "COEX Mall." *COEX Mall*, VisitSeoul.net,
   30 Apr. 2021, english.visitseoul.net/shopping/COEX-Mall_/271.

54 Perrault, Dominique. "Lightwalk Gangnam International Transit Center, Seoul." Dominique Perrault Architecte, 2017.
55 Seoul International District. "Hyundai GBC & Seoul Medical Center – Build a New Landmark in Seoul Where People Around the World Can Communicate and Share with Citizens of the City." *Hyundai Global Business Center (GBC) Site > Hyundai GBC & SEOUL Medical Center > SEOUL International District*, Seoul Metropolitan Government, 2020, sid.seoul.go.kr/front/en/pageView.do?page=%2Fhyundai%2Fhyundai.

5 Toward an Infra-Architectural Urbanism

The typological analysis of Seoul shows the potential role that architecture can take in organizing urbanization. The findings enforce the validity of architectural concepts from the second half of the 20th century regarding islands and megastructures as possible solutions for 21st century urbanization. This also suggests an infra-architectural hybrid model as an evolution in terminology, superseding megastructures, Structuralism, and Metabolist theory. Having typologies layered over time as demarcated architectural enclaves is perhaps a Seoul-specific urban phenomenon. Seoul's urban blocks are typological islands that serve distinct functions: housing, work, entertainment, culture, and so forth.

This offers an advancement on the concepts of O. M. Ungers's *Berlin: A Green Archipelago.*[1] The city can be read as an archipelago of typological islands that can be in dense proximity to each other while remaining autonomous offering the flexibility to have segmented developments. Typological islands in Seoul can also be monocultural or polycultural "micro-cities."

Nine typological islands were identified and labeled as urban blocks: political block, iconic block, apartment block, megaform block, superblock, tower block, deep block, cultural block, and podium block, each with its own particular characteristics.[2] Their mapping allows for a clearer identification of the urban morphology demonstrating a new reading of a megalopolis not through infrastructure but through architecture. This adds an extra layer of information and definition to urban mappings that previously only showed binary data of built versus unbuilt. It also shows the graphic representation of the city as a dense archipelago. The architectural island by itself is an autonomous element that produces the urban fabric, and hence the graphic style removes all the infrastructural elements to emphasize the architectural reading. Ungers used it as a mechanism to deal with a shrinking city effect to salvage and strengthen the remains of Berlin. In this case, the typological island works as an aggregation unit where each island is a subunit of the larger formation. As a subunit, it can be identified as having a particular set of parameters and qualities that can be adapted to other parts of the city. Understanding different case studies for each typology allows one to assume the behavior of the same typology in

DOI: 10.4324/9781032684963-5

a different part of the city. This adds a qualitative component to the reading of islands, aside from the quantitative factors that can also be extracted much easier.

Seoul has an archipelago structure of architectural typological islands aboveground that are connected by an infra-architectural hybrid typology. As previously mentioned, this typology does not form urban blocks, but it produces a macro urban fabric organizational structure. It answers the need for infrastructural commons to be formalized as the guiding urban framework, the need for new pedestrian grounds, and the dichotomy between the temporal and permanent metabolic evolution of a city.

Metro-centric policies like the Seoul Transportation Vision 2030 have reinforced the importance of subway station nodes and the use of the subway as the primary mode of transportation in Seoul. The subway stations themselves have become urban centers, mutating their morphology more like underground buildings rather than infrastructural platforms. Their connectivity to the neighborhoods they service has also provided viability for the stations to become prime commercial real estate and offer service programs. As primary entrances to neighborhoods, some stations have also been transformed into cultural gates that exhibit the history of the neighborhood reflecting their industry to promote local production as a cultural agenda. The underground system goes beyond the singular use of transportation infrastructure and serves more as a connected pedestrian layer of the city, separate from the vehicular layer. This makes the case for this system being analogous to a megastructure though there is a need for a variation or adaptation to the concept of "plug-in" units as presented by the Metabolist. In Maki's project for Mecca, the scale of a plug-in unit is that of a house, while my infra-architectural model proposes the typological island scale as the plug-in unit. These need to connect to the infra-architectural layer within a 10 minute walking radius. Some of the blocks are physically attached to the underground system while others are part of the system by proximity (have to be within the walking radius of a subway station exit). Tower blocks or deep blocks usually have a direct connection to the underground system developed by the private sector in order to give a direct access to the consumer.

The comparison of the Euljiro section to The Smithsons' Golden Lane over London, Constant's New Babylon over Amsterdam and Paris, and Paul Rudolph's LOMEX over Manhattan also presented a new variation for layering the city. While the avant-garde focused primarily on air rights for these expansive structures, the underground system is less obstructive. This allows for uninterrupted growth while connecting more sensitive areas of the city such as historically protected structures forming a new type of linear city based on the subway lines.

The dichotomy between bounded typological island units and an expansive infra-architectural hybrid layer that connects them also produces a clearer definition of "megacity," particularly for Seoul. This infra-architectural hybrid model presents Seoul as being a "city" rather than a nebulous conurbation, but rather than establishing "city" as a singular bounded form, Seoul presents an agglomeration of bounded subunits (micro-cities) that make up the megacity. Yet, this is also a hybrid model as the agglomeration of typological islands can also be incremental, and expansive through the infra-architectural layer making it a model for controlled urbanization. All of this, produces a very unique phenomenon where one can experience the city as a constant pairing between inside and outside, underground and aboveground, infrastructural linearity and architectural enclaves, perhaps summarized as infra-architectural urbanism and interior urbanism.

Theorizing an Infra-Architectural Urbanism and Interior Urbanism

Interior urbanism can be defined as the condition of urban growth as one continuous interior space. The concepts of metropolitan architecture have been summarized with the phrase "city within a city." For Ungers, this was the architectural island. For Koolhaas, this may have emerged from the effects of verticalism in Manhattan. In verticalism, Koolhaas theorized the possibility of congesting the phenomena of a city into a building through the stratification of programmatic layers in a skyscraper. This is possible through the use of technology that allows for an interior experience of multiple environments inside one building accessible through an elevator. For Seoul, the underground network and its typological island connections shift this interpretation from verticalism to horizontalism. Analogous to the skyscraper layering programs, and the elevator being the connector, the typological islands provide a variety of autonomous environments (layers in a skyscraper) connected by the subway (elevator in a skyscraper). A direct connection from the different blocks to the underground provides a continuous interior experience where a citizen can travel from an apartment building to a work building, or recreational social space without ever stepping outside. Although this may seem utopic or dystopic, it is a real possibility in Seoul. For example, the Twin City and Asterium apartment towers by Seoul Station connect directly underground to Line 1 and Line 4 taking you to Jongno Tower for work, Dongdaemun History and Culture park for entertainment, and Lotte Mart in Seoul Station for groceries. As more connections are made to the network, the city works as one horizontal megastructure building. This process could be compared to the Structuralist proposals by Alexis Josic, Georges Candilis, Shadrach Woods, and Manfred Schiedhelm for a "mat building" typology where a horizontal structure would serve as the connective framework and buildings could attach to it allowing for organic growth. The mat building was tested in the winning competition entry for the Freie Universität Berlin in 1962 and for the proposal of Frankfurt Römerberg in 1963. Differently from the Seoul underground, the mat building typology offered the possibility for buildings to plug-in at any point while the Seoul underground initially allowed connections based on station nodes. This is changing as the underground is expanding outside of the station nodes as is the case for the CBD.

The experience of the underground is becoming more similar to the intended use of the mat building. While Frankfurt Römerberg was not built, the built portion of the Freie Universität Berlin offers a perspective on the concept of the mat building. The Freie Universität Berlin proposed the idea for an adaptable mat building that could grow organically based on the needs and funding from the university. The framework relied on a system of interiorized roads to which the program could plug into. Much like the Metabolist, services were stationary and meant to have a permanence while the plug-ins could change over time. While the built structure does not follow the drawing presented during the competition, the idea remains and demonstrates the concept with the addition of a library by Norman Foster in 2005. The plug-ins can follow an autonomous architectural language and provide an additional interior experience to the overall mat building. In Seoul, the underground framework serves as the stationary common experience while the typological islands offer the autonomous environment, which are often interiorized.

The Freie Universität Berlin condenses the concept of interiorized streets as a singular mat building rather than an urban system, which was proposed one year later for Frankfurt Römerberg in 1963 also by Candilis, Josic, and Woods. For the reconstruction of the center of Frankfurt, the team proposed a megastructure with pedestrian decks at three levels that forms small blocks for the city to infill as needed. In Candilis's explanation, the complex would consist of a history museum, a museum and dance school, a library, youth center, exhibition hall, art galleries, cinema, cabaret, restaurants, offices, retail and convenience stores, cafes, and lodging.[3] The aim was to create a three-dimensional city that could adapt in time.

For Seoul, this is the condition being generated through the expanding underground system. The CBD underground is gradually becoming a grid to which buildings connect to through their basement programming. The subway, analogous to the elevator, allows for the user to move throughout an interior city, blending infrastructural space with architectural space, as well as public with private buildings. Understandably, the comparison of the entire Seoul underground to the Freie Universität is disproportionate as FU Berlin can be understood as one singular object, while the Seoul underground offers a variety of experiences and connections between underground and aboveground. The point is simply to express that the underground network is conceptualized as the new pedestrian street, similar to what Josic, Candilis, and Woods proposed. As the city of Seoul grew, public space was never developed as its own typology like the London Square or Italian Piazzas. Instead, the infrastructural space was always common ground. From the early days of Joseon, streets and alleyways were the only public spaces. Even today, streets under 12 m wide are appropriated as common space. Extensive research on this phenomenon was published as "Borrowed City" by Motoelastico, where they diagram the private and common use of the public space.[4]

As the subway system expanded and grew as an interiorized layer so did the public spaces associated with it. The interiorization of the public space linked to public transportation was theorized by Abalos and Herreors in their Hybrids essay for the COAM as an explanation for the hybridization between infrastructure and architecture being a symbiotic process mutually beneficial. This is true for Seoul where large commercial areas link directly to the subway exits. COEX, for example, renovated its interiors with larger public spaces such as an amphitheater and a library plaza. Jamsil station also renovated its underground with plazas that seamlessly transition into the Lotte World Mall and Lotte Tower. Yeongdeungpo exits into Times Square's plaza often used as an interiorized market. The same is true for public buildings like the new City Hall, which renovated its basement level as the citizens hall, connecting directly to exit 4 of Line 1.

Although spatial transitions are fluid, there is still a distinction between the root organizing system and the plug-in units which form the infra-architectural urbanization model beyond just the interiorization of the city. For Seoul, this consists of the underground network as the organizing system, while the typological islands above work as the plug-ins. Depending on the typology of the block island, it can directly plug-in the network through physical connections, which forms the interiorized urbanity. For example, COEX is directly connected to the Seolleung Station as exit 6 and Lotte World Mall connects to Jamsil Station. Jongno Tower (tower block) connects Jonggak Station, and City Hall to Line 2. Typological islands such as cultural blocks, and apartment blocks are connected through proximity via exits that are within a 600 m radius. There were pragmatic reasons for the resulting condition. Housing islands were driven by government policy in order to accommodate the growing population, or cultural islands came to be as a result of an urban policy to incentivize international exchange both economic and cultural. Some were driven through public–private partnerships such as COEX and Jamsil in order to develop extreme typologies while improving the public infrastructure, and through the Transport Vision 2030, the city promoted the subway network and pedestrian connectivity. Conceptually, no architectural physical connection exists between typological islands as they perform autonomously at ground level. Although it is possible to walk, or drive between islands on roads and sidewalks at ground level, the priority is to minimize the use of the car and prioritize the pedestrian experience. As the city moves with the Seoul 2030 vision for making a walkable, sustainable city, the infra-architectural layer will be the predominant layer for mobility and act as the commons for the city as distances between islands make it difficult to walk from one to the other.

The infra-architectural layer can also be compared to Tange's Metabolism, with the primary distinction being the architecture plug-in unit. While in projects like Tokyo Bay, or his plan for Mecca, Tange used smaller architectural buildings as the plug-in units, the architectural typological islands work as the plug-in unit instead. This provides larger variability of environments within a singular system, and has several implications in the understanding of large conurbations like Seoul:

1. It provides a basic formal strategy. For Seoul, this is a multi-linear city. Oswald Nagler had favored the linear model of urbanization when he was invited to Korea in the 1950s to revise the urbanization plans. For Nagler, a linear system allowed for flexibility in correlation to the necessary infrastructure. The plan was dismissed for radial planning leading to the 1966 plan of Seoul. Despite the rigorous radial planning though, I argue that the current organization of Seoul is highly linked to its subway lines. Density nodes are organized around the stations, and the subway aims to be the primary means of mobility. Hence, as a line extends, the city extends.

2. Through the multi-linear city strategy, Seoul presents the case for being a "city" rather than a nebulous conurbation. Architecture has a role in organizing the form of the city and its subunits. As previously discussed, the criticism for urbanism has been that infrastructure displaced architecture with the project of urbanization, making the architectural project for the city inert. Seoul presents an otherwise condition of being composed of multiple bounded architectural island units connected through an architectural megastructure. This reinforces the term "megacity" as an appropriate denomination for Seoul.

3. The multi-linear city presents a better condition for understanding megacities through quantitative and qualitative readings of the typological island subunits tied by the underground megastructure. In the existing condition of Seoul in which the expansion is happening both aboveground and underground, the islands are plug-in units regardless of the system plugging into them or the island plugging into the system. Typological islands can be analyzed through case studies to understand the general makeup of the same typology elsewhere in Seoul. This can be done through analysis of general data for demographics, geography, and local economies – data that is more readily available through the city's open Big Data platform and satellite imagery. These are similar methodologies used for a quantitative analysis of "cities" as a whole. Big Data can still be utilized for understanding the islands in terms of their use. Open-source software and code are also more accessible for artificial intelligence and machine learning to perform pattern recognition. This is being implemented in some cities for facial recognition, but this could also be used to recognize pedestrians, vehicles, bicycles, appropriations, signage, and building typologies within an island. Already Seoul is one of the world's most connected cities with an extensive CCTV network and digital monitoring through cell phones. Hence, it would be a next step in analyzing data that has already been created.

The recognition of island typologies and their qualitative parameters could be mapped out over time to understand the mutations of case studies, as the typology can be understood as behaving similarly in other parts of the city. While this model is specifically working in Seoul, it could potentially be utilized in developing cities that borrow the development model from Seoul incorporating island typologies linked to an underground network. For example, this is currently being proposed for a new linear city spanning 170 km in Saudi Arabia called "The Line" where cars will be omitted and an aboveground layer will be organized based on stations of the underground linear network.[5] While building new cities is a huge undertaking, the Seoul infra-architectural model perhaps presents a more sustainable way to organize existing conurbations.

Going back to the introductory question of what role can architecture take in a world guided by urbanization, perhaps architecture can be a primary organizing tool through typological urbanization of islands and megastructures.

Notes

1 Ungers, O. M., et al. *The City in the City: Berlin: A Green Archipelago.* Zurich: Lars Müller Publishers, 2013.
2 A brief description of this was also published in Topos Magazine. Luna, Rafael. "Insular Structures." *Munich, Topos*, no. 113, 2020, pp. 76–81.
3 Georges Candilis. *Bâtir la vie. Un architecte témoin de son temps.* Paris: Infolio Éditions, 2012, p. 231.
4 Bruno, Marco, et al. *Borrowed City: Private Use of Public Space in Seoul.* Seoul: Damdi Publishing, 2015.
5 "The Line." *NEOM*, 2021, www.neom.com/en-us/whatistheline.

Bibliography

"68% of the World Population Projected to Live in Urban Areas by 2050, Says UN | UN Desa Department of Economic and Social Affairs." *United Nations*, United Nations, 16 May 2018, www.un.org/development/desa/en/news/population/2018-revision-of-world-urbanization-prospects.html.

Abalos, Iñaki, and Juan Herreros. "Híbridos." *Arquitectura COAM*, vol. 290, 1992.

"About Deoksugung Palace." *Deoksugung*, Cultural Heritage Administration, http://deoksugung.go.kr/en/c/about/2.

"About the World Trade Center Seoul: WTC Seoul." *About the World Trade Center Seoul | WTC Seoul*, www.wtcseoul.com/eng/introduce/intro02.do.

Allen, Stan. *Points + Lines: Diagrams and Projects for the City*. New York: Princeton Architectural Press, 2012.

Angel, Schlomo. "[Re]Form: New Investigations in Urban Form, Panel 2." *YouTube*, Harvard Graduate School of Design, 26 Sept. 2018, https://youtu.be/a2RaiAORKks.

Annals of King Taejo. *Chapter 6, 13th day of 8th month, 1394*. Seoul: Seoul Museum of History.

Architecture, Dominique Perrault. "Dominique Perrault Architecture." *Dominique Perrault Architecture – LIGHTWALK – Gangnam Intermodal Transit Center, Seoul*, www.perraultarchitecture.com/en/projects/3463-lightwalk_-_gangnam_intermodal_transit_center_seoul.html.

Argan, Giulio Carlo. "On the Typology of Architecture." *Theorizing a New Agenda for Architecture: An Anthology of Architectural Theory, 1965– 1995*, edited by Kate Nesbitt. New York: Princeton Architectural Press, 1996, pp. 242–246.

Atlas of Urban Expansion, 2016, http://atlasofurbanexpansion.org/.

"Atlas of Urban Expansion." *Atlas of Urban Expansion – Cities*, 2016, www.atlasofurbanexpansion.org/data.

Aureli, Pier Vittorio. *The Possibility of an Absolute Architecture*. Cambridge, MA: MIT Press, 2011.

Avermaete, Tom. "Candilis-Josic-Woods Free University Berlin." *HIC Arquitectura*. Rotterdam: NAi Publishers, 2021, hicarquitectura.com/2017/12/georges-candilis-free-university-berlin/#gallery-2.

"Bank of Korea Money Museum, National Historic Site No. 280." *Bank of Korea*, 한국은행, www.bok.or.kr/eng/main/contents.do?menuNo=400265.

Bastlund, Knud, and Siegfried Giedion. *José Luis Sert: Architecture, City Planning, Urban Design*. New York: Praeger, 1967, p. 52.

Bekaert, Geert, et al. *After-Sprawl: Research for the Contemporary City*. Edited by Xaveer De Geyter. Rotterdam: NAi Publishers, 2002.

Belogolovsky, Vladimir. "Interview with Yona Friedman: 'Imagine, Having Improvised Volumes "Floating" in Space, Like Balloons'." *ArchDaily*, ArchDaily, 24 Feb. 2020, https://tinyurl.com/3js9nv99.

Berrone, Pascual, and Joan Enric Ricart, editors. *IESE Cities in Motion Index*. University of Navarra, Navarra, Spain, 2016.

Beuchert, Tobias. "The Urban Morphology on Our Planet – Global Perspectives from Space." *Medium*, Urban AI, 6 Apr. 2022, https://medium.com/urban-ai/the-urban-morphology-on-our-planet-global-perspectives-from-space-ce9027a51064.

Bratton, Benjamin H. *The Stack – on Software and Sovereignty*. Cambridge, MA: MIT Press, 2016.

Brenner, Neil. "Debating Planetary Urbanization: For an Engaged Pluralism." *Environment and Planning D: Society and Space*, vol. 36, no. 3, 2018, pp. 570–590. https://doi.org/10.1177/0263775818757510.

Brillembourg, Alfredo, and Hubert Klumpner. *Infrastructure as Architecture: Designing Composite Networks*. Edited by Katrina Stoll and Scott Lloyd. Berlin: Jovis, 2010, pp. 26–35.

Bruegmann, Robert. "Paul Rudolph's Strange Vision of a Cross-Manhattan Expressway (and Other Unfinished Projects)." *Literary Hub*. Princeton Architectural Press, 5 Jan. 2020, https://tinyurl.com/49k5cnft.

Bruegmann, Robert, and Paul Rudolph. "Interview with Paul Rudolph/ Interviewed by Robert Bruegmann, Compiled Under the Auspices of the Chicago Architects Oral History Project, the Ernest R. Graham Study Center for Architectural Drawings, Department of Architecture, the Art Institute of Chicago." *Chicago Architects Oral History Project*, 1993, pp. 1–66.

Bruno, Marco, et al. *Borrowed City: Private Use of Public Space in Seoul*. Seoul: Damdi Publishing, 2015.

"Buildings & Projects." *Paul Rudolph Foundation*, https://paulrudolph.org/buildings-projects/.

Burdett, Ricky, and Deyan Sudjic. *The Endless City*. New York: Phaidon Press Limited, 2010.

"Category: Japanese General Government Building in Korea." *Wikimedia Commons*, 27 Aug. 2006, https://commons.wikimedia.org/wiki/Category:Japanese_General_Government_Building_in_Korea.

Center for International Affairs. "Seoul – 4.1 Population Growth and Expansion of the Urban Center." *Seoul – 4.1 Population Growth and Expansion of the Urban Center – CefiaWiki*, Center for International Affairs, 19 Jan. 2017, http://cefia.aks.ac.kr:84/index.php?title=Seoul_-_4.1_Population_Growth_and_Expansion_of_the_Urban_Center.

Cerdá Ildefonso. *Teoría General De La urbanización y aplicación De Sus Principios y Doctrinas a La Reforma y Ensanche De Barcelona*, vol. 1. Madrid: Imprenta Española, 1867.

Christiaanse, Kees, et al. *The Grand Projet: Understanding the Making and Impact of Urban Megaprojects*. Rotterdam: Nai010 Publishers, 2019.

Competition Organizing Committee, Gwanghwamun Square Project Group. "International Design Competition for New Gwanghwamun Square." 새로운 광화문광장 조성 설계공모, Seoul Metropolitan Government, 2018, https://project.seoul.go.kr/view/viewDetailArch.do?cpttMstSeq=229.

Conrads, Ulrich, editor. *Programs and Manifestoes on 20th Century Architecture*. Cambridge, MA: MIT Press, 1971.

"Creation of Industrial Ecosystem for Smart City." *Policy Tasks < Digital Seoul*, Seoul Metropolitan Government, 2021, digital.seoul.go.kr/eng/smart-seoul/policy-tasks/smart-economy.

Cronon, William. "The Trouble with Wilderness: Or, Getting Back to the Wrong Nature." *Environmental History*, vol. 1, no. 1, Jan. 1996, pp. 7–28.

Cuff, Dana. "Architecture as Public Work." *Infrastructure as Architecture: Designing Composite Networks*, edited by Katrina Stoll and Scott Lloyd. Berlin: Jovis, 2010, pp. 18–25.

Cultural Heritage Administration of Korea. *Main Palace: Center of Power, Politics, Economy, and Culture*. Cultural Heritage Administration of Korea, Daejeon, South Korea, 2011.

Cunha Borges, João, and Teresa Marat-Mendes. "Walking on Streets-in-the-Sky: Structures for Democratic Cities." *Journal of Aesthetics & Culture*, vol. 11, no. 1, 2019, pp. 1–15. https://doi.org/10.1080/20004214.2019.1596520.

Den, Heuvel Dirk van, et al. *Alison and Peter Smithson: From the House of the Future to a House of Today*. Rotterdam: 010 Publishers, 2004.

Department of Economic and Social Affairs Population Division. *World Urbanization Prospects The 2018 Revision*. United Nations, 2019, pp. 1–103.

"Dewitt Chestnut Apartments." *SOM*, 11 Oct. 2021, www.som.com/projects/dewitt_chestnut_apartments.

D'Hooghe, Alexander. "Transportation Infrastructure as Our Commons." *Infrastructural Monument*. New York: Princeton Architectural Press, 2016, pp. 15–20.

Dominique Perrault Architecture. "Dominique Perrault Architecture." *Dominique Perrault Architecture – LIGHTWALK – Gangnam Intermodal Transit Center, Seoul*, www.perraultarchitecture.com/en/projects/3463-lightwalk_-_gangnam_intermodal_transit_center_seoul.html.

Doxiadis, C. A., and J. G. Papaioannou. *Ecumenopolis: The Inevitable City of the Future*. New York: Norton, 1975.

Easterling, Keller. *Extrastatecraft: The Power of Infrastructure Space*. London: Verso, 2016.

ESCAP. *Urbanization Trends in Asia and the Pacific*. United Nations, Nov. 2013, www.unescap.org/sites/default/files/SPPS-Factsheet-urbanization-v5.pdf.

European Capitals of Culture – European Commission, https://ec.europa.eu/culture/sites/default/files/capitals-culture-candidates-guide_en_vdec17.pdf.

Fenton, Joseph. *Hybrid Buildings*. New York: Pamphlet Architecture, 1985.

Finger, Matthias. "2–5 Interview with Mr. Christoph Rothballer – BCG – Block 2 – Introduction to Principles of Urban Infrastructure Management." *Coursera*, École Polytechnique Fédérale De Lausanne, 2017, www.coursera.org/learn/managing-urban-infrastructures-1/lecture/c4ziS/2-5-interview-with-mr-christoph-rothballer-bcg.

Frampton, Adam, et al. *Cities Without Ground: A Hong Kong Guidebook.* Navato, CA: Oro Editions, 2012.

Frampton, Kenneth. "The Generic Street as a Continuous Built Form." *On Streets,* edited by Stanford Anderson. Cambridge, MA: MIT Press, 1986, pp. 308–337.

Frampton, Kenneth, and Alison Smithson. "Team 10 Primer." *Leonardo,* vol. 2, no. 2, 1969, p. 201. http://doi.org/10.2307/1572031.

"Frank Lloyd Wright and the City: Density vs. Dispersal: Moma." *The Museum of Modern Art,* www.moma.org/calendar/exhibitions/1410.

Friedman, Yona. *Yona Friedman: Pro Domo.* Barcelona: ACTAR, 2006.

Garnier, Tony, and Riccardo Mariani. *Tony Garnier: Une Cite Industrielle.* New York: Rizzoli International Publications, 1990.

Georges Candilis. *Bâtir la vie. Un architecte témoin de son temps.* Paris: Infolio Éditions, 2012.

Ghosh, Iman. "70 Years of Urban Growth in 1 Dazzling Infographic." *World Economic Forum,* 3 Sept. 2019, www.weforum.org/agenda/2019/09/mapped-the-dramatic-global-rise-of-urbanization-1950-2020/.

"GHSL – Global Human Settlement Layer." *Global Human Settlement – Degree of Urbanisation – European Commission,* 6 July 2016, https://ghsl.jrc.ec.europa.eu/CFS.php.

Global Human Settlement – Atlas of the Human Planet 2016 Overview – European Commission, 6 July 2016, https://ghsl.jrc.ec.europa.eu/documents/Atlas_2016.pdf.

Golubeva, Yana, et al. *Undiscovered St. Petersburg.* St. Petersburg: MLA+, 2018.

Graham, Edward Montgomery. "The Miracle with a Dark Side: Korean Economic Development Under Park Chung Hee." *Reforming Korea's Industrial Conglomerates.* Washington, DC: Inst. for International Economics, 2005, pp. 11–50.

Graham, Stephen. "Introduction: Cities and Infrastructure Networks." *International Journal of Urban and Regional Research,* vol. 24, no. 1, Mar. 2000, pp. 114–119.

"Gyeongbokgung." Edited by Center for International Affairs, /Images/Thumb/d/Db/UKS04_SEOUL_IMG_117.JPG/, Center for International Affairs, http://cefia.aks.ac.kr:84/images/thumb/d/db/UKS04_Seoul_img_117.jpg/.

Henry, Todd A. *Assimilating Seoul: Japanese Rule and the Politics of Public Space in Colonial Korea, 1910–1945.* Berkeley: University of California Press, 2016.

Hertzberger, Herman. *Architecture and Structuralism: The Ordering of Space.* Edited by Els Brinkman. Translated by John Kirkpatrick. Rotterdam: Nai010 Publishers, 2015.

Hilberseimer, Ludwig. *The New City Principles of Planning.* Charleston: Nabu Press, 2014.

Hilberseimer, Ludwig, et al. *Metropolisarchitecture and Selected Essays.* New York: GSAPP Books, 2012.

"The History and Definition of 'Infrastructure'." *Merriam-Webster,* Merriam-Webster, www.merriam-webster.com/words-at-play/infrastructure-history-definition.

"History of KEPCO." *Kepco*, https://home.kepco.co.kr/kepco/EN/A/htmlView/ENAAHP002.do?menuCd=EN010102.

Howard, Ebenezer, et al. *Garden Cities of to-Morrow*. Cambridge, MA: The MIT Press, 2007.

Huh, Donghyun, and Vladimir Tikhonov. "The Korean Courtiers' Observation Mission's Views on Meiji Japan and Projects of Modern State Building." *Korean Studies*, vol. 29, no. 1, 2005, pp. 30–54. https://doi.org/10.1353/ks.2006.0004.

Hwang, Kyung Moon. "State Making Under Imperialism: Fragmentation and Consolidation in the Central State." *Rationalizing Korea the Rise of the Modern State, 1894–1945*. Oakland, CA: University of California Press, 2016, pp. 25–51.

"Hybrids I. High-Rise Mixed-Use Buildings." Alava: a+t Architecture Publishers, 2008, https://aplust.net/tienda/revistas/Serie%20HYBRIDS/HYBRIDS%20I.%20H%C3%ADbridos%20verticales/.

Hyundai Department Store Group History, www.ehyundai.com/newPortal/group/GI/GI000002.do.

Infrastructural Monument. New York: Princeton Architectural Press, 2016.

Jeon, Wu-Yong. *The Seoul City Wall: Walking the History of Seoul*. Seoul: The Seoul Institute, 2018.

Jung, Inha. *Architecture and Urbanism in Modern Korea*. Honolulu: University of Hawaii Press, 2014.

Kaijima, Momoyo, et al. *Made in Tokyo*. Tokyo: Kajima Institute Publishing Co., Ltd., 2021.

Kang, Hong-bin, editor. *History of Seoul: Seoul Museum of History, Places and Memories*. Seoul: Seoul Museum of History, 2014.

Kang, Hong-bin, editor. *Seoul Museum of History: Places and Memories*. Seoul: Seoul Museum of History, 2013.

Kawazoe, Noboru, et al. *Metabolism: The Proposals for a New Urbanism*. Tokyo: Bijutsu Shuppansha, 1960.

Kim, Jae-Eun. "Gojong, a Misfortunate Monarch." *Korean Heritage*, vol. 42, 2018, pp. 8–15.

Kim, Joochul, and Sang-Chuel Choe. *Seoul: The Making of a Metropolis*. Chichester: Wiley, 1997.

Kim, Kwang-jung. *Seoul, Twentieth Century, Growth and Change of the Last 100 Years*. Seoul: Seoul Development Institute, 2003.

Kim, Mun Taek, editor. *Seoul Museum of History: Places and Memories*. Seoul: Seoul Museum of History, 2013.

Kim, Seungjun. "[Metro] a Driving Force for Sustainable Development and REMARKABLE Change, Seoul METROPOLITAN SUBWAY." 서울정책 아카이브 *Seoul Solution*, City of Seoul, 10 Nov. 2016, seoulsolution.kr/en/node/1802.

Kim, Seungjun, and Joonho Ko. *Seoul's Light-Rail Projects Driven by Private Investment for Poorly Serviced Areas*. Seoul: Seoul Institute, 2017, pp. 229–238.

Kim, Sungbae. *Korea's Confucian Strategies Toward China During the Qing Dynasty and Their Implications*. Seoul: The East Asia Institute, 2013.

Kim, Sun-Wung. "The Land Readjustment Program." 서울정책아카이브 *Seoul Solution*, The Seoul Institute, 26 Apr. 2017, https://seoulsolution.kr/en/node/3446.

Kim, Sun-Wung. "Urban Planning & Management." 서울정책아카이브 *Seoul Solution*, 31 Aug. 2017, www.seoulsolution.kr/en/node/3441.

Kinkela, David. "The Ecological Landscapes of Jane Jacobs and Rachel Carson." *American Quarterly*, vol. 61, no. 4, 2009, pp. 905–928. https://doi.org/10.1353/aq.0.0115.

Kipnis, Jeffrey. "Jeffrey Kipnis – in Praise of Sloth, Indolence and All Other Forms of Torpor." *YouTube*, Architectural Association, 9 Oct. 2015, https://youtu.be/sEWLRDdD-dA.

Kirschner, Marc, and John Gerhart. *The Plausibility of Life: Great Leaps of Evolution*. New Haven, CT: Yale University Press, 2005.

Ko, Joonho. "A Guide to Transportation Policy (General)." 서울정책아카이브 *Seoul Solution*, Seoul Institute, 10 Feb. 2017, www.seoulsolution.kr/en/content/guide-transportation-policy-general.

Ko, Joonho. "Seoul Transport Vision 2030." *Urban Solutions*, no. 6, Feb. 2015, pp. 28–35.

Koolhaas, Rem. "The City of the Captive Globe." *The City of the Captive Globe*, 1 Jan. 1972, https://dome.mit.edu/handle/1721.3/21258.

Koolhaas, Rem. *Delirious New York: A Retroactive Manifesto for Manhattan*. New York: Monacelli, 1994.

Koolhaas, Rem. "'Life in the Metropolis' or 'The Culture of Congestion'." *Architectural Design*, May 1977, pp. 319–325.

Koolhaas, Rem, and Bruce Mau. *S, M, L, XL*. New York: Monacelli Press, 1998.

Koolhaas, Rem, and Hans Ulrich Obrist. *Project Japan Metabolism Talks*. Cologne: Taschen GmbH, 2011, p. 106.

Korail. "KORAIL." 코레일, info.korail.com/mbs/www/subview.jsp?id=www_020203010000.

"Korea Land & Housing Corporation." *Lh.or.kr*, Korea Land and Housing Corporation, www.lh.or.kr/eng/contents/cont.do.

"Korea – Rossetti, Carlo." *Sothebys.com*, www.sothebys.com/en/auctions/ecatalogue/2015/travel-atlases-maps-natural-history-l15405/lot.173.html.

KYUNGBANG CO, LTD. "Korea's No. 1 Shopping Complex Times Square." *TIMESSQUARE > about Us*, KYUNGBANG CO, LTD, 2022, www.timessquare.co.kr/?controller=eng&action=about.

Lee, Hyang A. "Tracing Seoul's Modernity: The History of Urban Planning in Colonial Seoul." *Cross-Currents: East Asian History and Culture Review*, no. 27, June 2018, pp. 208–214.

"Lotte." *Lotte.co.kr*, www.lotte.co.kr/global/en/business/compDetail.do?compCd=L201.

Luna, Rafael. "10 Architectural Typologies in Seoul." *SPACE*, no. 626, Jan. 2020, pp. 34–41.

Luna, Rafael. "Informal Annexations." *Intar Journal*, vol. 10, 2019, pp. 6–13.

Luna, Rafael. "The Infrastructural Interior: Interior Urbanism Through the Infra-Architectural Hybrid." *Inner Magazine*, no. 3, Dec. 2018, pp. 43–51.

Luna, Rafael. "Insular Structures." *Topos*, no. 113, Dec. 2020, pp. 76–81.

Lee, Christopher C. M., and Sam Jacoby. "Typological Urbanism and the Idea of the City." *Architectural Design*, vol. 81, no. 1, 2011, pp. 14–23. https://doi.org/10.1002/ad.1184.

Lee, Christopher C. M., and Sam Jacoby. *Typological Urbanism: Projective Cities*. Chichester: Wiley, 2011.

"The Line." *NEOM*, 2021, www.neom.com/en-us/whatistheline.

Maki, Fumihiko. *Investigations in Collective Form*. School of Architecture, Washington University, St Louis, MO, 1964.

Maki, Fumihiko, and Masato Ohtaka. *Some Thoughts on Collective Form; with an Introduction to Group-Form*. St Louis: Washington University, 1961.

"Management Policies for Seoul City Center & Changes." 서울정책아카이브 *Seoul Solution*, 10 Feb. 2017, https://seoulsolution.kr/en/node/3442.

"Management Policies for Seoul City Center & Changes." 서울정책아카이브 *Seoul Solution*, 10 Feb. 2017, https://seoulsolution.kr/en/content/management-policies-seoul-city-center-changes.

Map (에스맵), 2022, http://smap.seoul.go.kr/.

McDonough, Thomas F. "Situationist Space." *October*, vol. 67, 1994, pp. 58–77.

McDonough, Tom. *The Activist Drawing: Retracing Situationist Architectures from Constant's New Babylon to Beyond*, edited by Zegher M. Catherine De and Mark Wigley. Cambridge, MA: The MIT Press, 2001, pp. 93–104.

"Megacities Worldwide | UNESCO." *Second International Conference on Water, Megacities and Global Change*, UNESCO, 2021, https://en.unesco.org/events/eaumega2021/megacities.

"Megastructures 1." Performance by Reyner Banham, *AA School*, Artnet, 15 Oct. 1974, www.aaschool.ac.uk/publicprogramme/whatson/megastructures-1.

Metro, and Seungjun Kim. *Construction of the Seoul Metro – the Driver Behind Sustainable Urban Growth & Change*. The Seoul Institute, Seoul, South Korea, 2017, pp. 193–205.

Min, Hyeon-Seok. "Sewun Mall Development Plan." 서울정책아카이브 *Seoul Solution*, 25 Sept. 2017, https://seoulsolution.kr/en/node/6304.

Moneo, Rafael. "On Typology." *A Journal for Ideas and Criticism in Architecture*, vol. 18. Cambridge, MA: MIT Press, 1978, pp. 23–45.

Moussavi, Farshid, and Michael Kubo. *The Function of Ornament*. Actar, 2008.

NASA, and NOAA. "Earth at Night." *NASA, NASA/NOAA*, Barcelona, Spain, 2 Apr. 2009, www.nasa.gov/sites/default/files/images/324350main_11_full.jpg. Accessed 17 May 2022.

New Office Construction Team at Jongno-gu Office. "The New Jongno-Gu Government Complex Design Competition." 종로구 통합청사 설계공모, Seoul Metropolitan Government, 2020, https://project.seoul.go.kr/view/viewDetailArch.do?cpttMstSeq=317.

Nieuwenhuys, Constant. "Constant's New Babylon on Permanent Display." *Kunstmuseum Den Haag*, 1 Oct. 2019, www.kunstmuseum.nl/en/constants-new-babylon-permanent-display.

Nieuwenhuys, Constant. "New Babylon-Amsterdam [I]." *Fondation Constant/Stichting Constant*, Fondation Constant, 3 Mar. 2022, https://stichtingconstant.nl/work/new-babylon-amsterdam-i.

Nieuwenhuys, Constant. "New Babylon-Paris." *Fondation Constant/Stichting Constant*, Fondation Constant, 6 Nov. 2020, https://stichtingconstant.nl/work/new-babylon-paris.

No, Chung-guk. *Seoul: A Journey Through 2000 Years of History*. The City History Compilation Committee of Seoul, Seoul, South Korea, 2009.

Park, Jinhee, and John Hong. *Convergent Flux: Contemporary Architecture and Urbanism in Korea*. Basel: Birkhäuser, 2012.

Park, Moonho. *The Understanding Korea Series (UKS) 4 Seoul*. Edited by The Center for International Affairs. Seongnam: The Academy of Korean Studies Press, 2015, p. 36.

Park, Young-Sin. "The Choson Industrial Exposition of 1915." *Binghamton University State University of New York*. ProQuest LLC, Ann Arbor, MI, 2019, pp. 1–461.

Patterson, Leanne, and Jae-Yong Jang, editors. *Seoul: A Journey Through 2000 Years of History*. The City History Compilation Committee of Seoul, Seoul, South Korea, 2009.

Pedret, Annie. "Aix-En-Provence (France) 19–26 July 1953 CIAM IX: Discussing the Charter of Habitat." *Team 10*, www.team10online.org/team10/meetings/1953-Aix.htm.

Picon, Antoine. *Smart Cities: A Spatialised Intelligence*. Chichester: Wiley, 2015.

"Population – New York City Population." *Planning-Population-NYC Population Facts – DCP*, www1.nyc.gov/site/planning/planning-level/nyc-population/population-facts.page#:~:text=New%20York%20has%20the%20highest,27%2C000%20people%20per%20square%20mile.

Quincy, Quatremère de. *Dictionnaire Historique D'architecture*. Paris: Librairie D'Adrien Le Clere, 1832, p. 629.

"Rapporti Bilaterali." *Seoul*, 12 Jan. 2022, https://ambseoul.esteri.it/ambasciata_seoul/it/i-rapporti-bilaterali/i-rapporti-bilaterali.html.

Rion, Gilles. "The Naked City, 1957." *Frac Centre*, 2022, www.frac-centre.fr/_en/art-and-architecture-collection/debord-guy/the-naked-city-317.html?authID=53&ensembleID=705.

Ritchie, Hannah, and Max Roser. "Urbanization." *Our World in Data*, 13 June 2018, https://ourworldindata.org/urbanization.

Roberts, Rebecca, et al. *Moma Highlights: 375 Works from the Museum of Modern Art, New York*. New York: Museum of Modern Art, 2019.

Rossetti, Carlo. *Corea e Coreani: Impressioni e Ricerche sull' Impero del Gran Han*. Bergamo: Instituto Italiano D'Arti Grafiche – Editore, 1905.

Rossi, Aldo. *The Architecture of the City*. Cambridge, MA: MIT Press, 2007.

Rowe, Colin, and Fred Koetter. *Collage City*. Basel: Birkhäuser, 2009.

Rudolph, Paul. "Lower Manhattan Expressway, New York City. Map Showing Proposed Development." *Library of Congress*, Library of Congress Prints and Photographs Division Washington, DC, 1967, loc.gov/pictures/resource/ppmsca.24382/.

Rudolph, Paul. *Lower Manhattan Expressway Section Perspective*. Library of Congress. www.loc.gov/item/2010648302/.

Ryon, Gilles. "The Naked City, 1957." *Frac Centre*, www.frac-centre.fr/_en/art-and-architecture-collection/debord-guy/the-naked-city-317.html?authID=53&ensembleID=705.

Santos, Sabrina. "Open Call: Sejong-Daero Historic Cultural Space Design Competition." *ArchDaily*, ArchDaily, 11 Aug. 2015, www.archdaily.com/771508/open-call-sejong-daero-historic-cultural-space-design-competition.

Sbriglio, Jacques. *Le Corbusier: L'unité D'habitation De Marseille Et Les Autres unités D'habitation à rezé-Les-Nantes, Berlin, Briey En forêt Et Firminy = unité D'habitation in Marseilles and the Four Other unité Blocks in rezé-Les-Nantes, Berlin, Briey En forêt and Firminy*. Fondation Le Corbusier, Birkhauser, Basel, 2004.

Sbriglio, Jacques, et al. *L'unité D'habitation De Marseille: Le Corbusier*. Ed. Parenthèses, Marseille, France, 1992.

"Seodaemun Prison History Hall." *Seodaemun Prison History Hall*, Seodaemungu City Management Corporation, www.sscmc.or.kr/foreign/eng/introduction.html.

"Seoul – 2.3 Population Changes in Hanseong." *Seoul – 2.3 Population Changes in Hanseong – CefiaWiki*, 19 Jan. 2017, http://cefia.aks.ac.kr:84/index.php?title=Seoul_-_2.3_Population_Changes_in_Hanseong.

"Seoul – 4.1 Population Growth and Expansion of the Urban Center." *Seoul – 4.1 Population Growth and Expansion of the Urban Center – CefiaWiki*, 19 Jan. 2017, http://cefia.aks.ac.kr:84/index.php?title=Seoul_-_4.1_Population_Growth_and_Expansion_of_the_Urban_Center.

"Seoul Guided Walking Tour." *Seoul Underground – A Different Plane of Time*, Seoul Tourism Organization, 27 Aug. 2020, english.visitseoul.net/walking-tour/Seoul-Underground/34964?letterSn=1822<content=200908_Seoul+Underground%3Cbr%3EA+Different+Plane+of+Time.

The Seoul Institute. "Global Zone Map." *The Seoul Research Data Service*, The Seoul Institute, 2008, https://data.si.re.kr/sites/default/files/2008-BR-01_12_%EA%B8%80%EB%A1%9C%EB%B2%8C%EC%A1%B4%20%EB%8C%80%EC%83%81%EC%A7%80%EC%97%AD%20EC%9C%84%EC%B9%98%EB%8F%84.jpg. Accessed 29 May 2022.

The Seoul Institute, Metro Policy, and Seungjun Kim. *Construction of the Seoul Metro – The Driver Behind Sustainable Urban Growth & Change*. Seoul: The Seoul Institute, 2017, pp. 193–205, p. 195.

The Seoul Institute, Urban Planning, and Hyeon-Seok Min. *Sewun Mall Development Plan*. Seoul: Seoul Metropolitan Government, 2017, pp. 1–11.

The Seoul Institute, Urban Planning, and Sun-Wung Kim. *Urban Planning & Management*. Seoul: Seoul Metropolitan Government, 2017, pp. 1–20.

Seoul International District. "Hyundai GBC & Seoul Medical Center – Build a New Landmark in Seoul Where People Around the World Can Communicate and Share with Citizens of the City." *Hyundai Global Business Center (GBC) Site > Hyundai GBC & SEOUL Medical Center > SEOUL International District*. Seoul Metropolitan Government, 2020, sid.seoul.go.kr/front/en/pageView.do?page=%2Fhyundai%2Fhyundai.

Seoul Metro. "Intro to Seoul Metro: Overview and History." *Seoul Metro*, 2017, www.seoulmetro.co.kr/en/page.do?menuIdx=653.

Seoul Metro Art Center, Seoul Tourism Organization, 29 Apr. 2019, english.visitseoul.net/attractions/Seoul-Metro-Art-Center-en_/29325.

"Seoullo7017Skygarden." *MVRDV*, www.mvrdv.nl/projects/208/seoullo-7017-skygarden.

서울교통공사. 서울교통공사, www.seoulmetro.co.kr/kr/board.do?menuIdx =548.

"서울의 통계." 서울시 정보소통광장, Seoul Institute, 2021, opengov. seoul.go.kr/stat.

Seoul Metropolitan Government. *Into SEOUL*. Seoul: Seoul Metropolitan Government, 2020.

Seoul Metropolitan Government. "Seoul's Competitiveness." *Seoul Metropolitan Government*, SMG, https://english.seoul.go.kr/city-hall/the-ranking-of-seoul/seouls-competitiveness/.

Seoul Metropolitan Government. "Seoul's New Gwanghwamun to Return to the Citizens in 2021 with Announcement of International Design Competition Winners -." *Seoul Metropolitan Government*, 24 Jan. 2019, http://english.seoul.go.kr/seouls-new-gwanghwamun-to-return-to-the-citizens-in-2021/#:~:text=Urban%20Planning%20News-,Seoul%27s%20New%20Gwanghwamun%20to%20Return%20to%20the%20Citizens%20in%202021,of%20International%20Design%20Competition%20Winners&text=Gwanghwamun%20Square%20will%20be%20returned,democratic%20space%20with%20treasured%20historicity.

Seoul Solution. "1. Cheonggyecheon (Stream) Restoration." 서울정책아카이브 *Seoul Solution*, 28 Sept. 2017, www.seoulsolution.kr/en/content/7475.

Seoul Solution. "Development of Gangnam." 서울정책아카이브 *Seoul Solution*, 12 Dec. 2017, www.seoulsolution.kr/en/node/3445.

Seoul Solution. "[Inclusive Growth] Sharing City Seoul Project." 서울정책아카이브 *Seoul Solution*, 28 June 2017, https://seoulsolution.kr/en/content/inclusive-growth-sharing-city-seoul-project.

Seoul Solution. "Management Policies for Seoul City Center & Changes." 서울정책아카이브 *Seoul Solution*, 10 Feb. 2017, https://seoulsolution.kr/en/content/management-policies-seoul-city-center-changes.

Seoul Solution. "Sewun Mall Development Plan." 서울정책아카이브 *Seoul Solution*, 25 Sept. 2017, https://seoulsolution.kr/en/node/6304.

Seoul Solution. "Urbanization Planning of Seoul." 서울정책아카이브 *Seoul Solution*, 30 Aug. 2021, https://seoulsolution.kr/en/node/2375.

Seoul Solution. "Vision 2030 for a Pedestrian-Friendly Seoul." 서울정책아카이브 *Seoul Solution*, Seoul Solution, 18 Nov. 2016, seoulsolution.kr/en/node/1769.

"Seoul's New Gwanghwamun to Return to the Citizens in 2021 with Announcement of International Design Competition Winners." *Urban Planning News*, Seoul Metropolitan Government, Jan. 2019, https://tinyurl.com/4kb3pb5v. Accessed 15 Apr. 2022.

Seoul Tourism Organization. "COEX Mall." *COEX Mall*, VisitSeoul.net, 30 Apr. 2021, english.visitseoul.net/shopping/COEX-Mall_/271.

"Seoul Transportation Corporation Subway Shopping Malls." 서울열린데이터광장, Seoul Transportation Corporation, 3 June 2020, data.seoul.go.kr/dataList/OA-12927/F/1/datasetView.do.

"Seoul Transportation Vision 2030 -." *Official Website of The*, 5 Oct. 2016, english.seoul.go.kr/policy/traffic/seoul-transportation-vision-2030/.

Sert, Josep Lluis. *Centres of Community Life*. Hoddesdon: CIAM 8 Conference, 1951.

Sert, Josep Lluis. "The Human Scale in City Planning." *New Architecture and City Planning: A Symposium*, edited by Paul Zucker. New York: Philosophical Library, 1971, pp. 392–412.

Sherman, Roger. "Battery Power: Recharging Architecture's Cause and Effect." *Infrastructural Monument*. New York: Princeton Architectural Press, 2016, p. 85.

Shinsegae Central City, http://eng.shinsegaecentralcity.com/about#:~:text= 'Shinsegae%20Central%20City'%20is%20Korea's,Bus%20Terminal%20 Co.%2C%20Ltd.

Simbirtseva, Tatiana, and Svetlana Levoshko. "Russian Architect Afanasy Seredin-Sabatin (1860–1921) in Korea: At the Roots of Modernity." *Institute of Theory of Architecture and Urban Planning*. Institute of Theory of Architecture and Urban Planning, St. Petersburg, Russia, 2017, pp. 1–13.

Smithson, Alison Margaret, and Peter Smithson. *The Charged Void: Architecture*. London: Monacelli Press, 2002, p. 84.

Smithson, Alison Margaret, and Peter Smithson. *The Charged Void, Urbanism*. London: Monacelli Press, 2005.

Smithson, Alison Margaret, and Peter Smithson. *Ordinariness and Light: Urban Theories 1952–1960 and Their Application in a Building Project 1963–1970*. MIT Press, Cambridge, MA, 1970.

Söderqvist, Lisbeth. "Structuralism in Architecture: A Definition." *Journal of Aesthetics & Culture*, vol. 3, no. 1, 2011, p. 5414, p. 2, http://doi.org/10.3402/ jac.v3i0.5414.

Song, In-ho. *Maps of Old Seoul*. Seoul: Seoul Museum of History, 2016.

Song, Kue-jin. "Transformation of the Dualistic International Order into the Modern Treaty System in the Sino-Korean Relationship." *International Journal of Korean History*, vol. 15, no. 2, Aug. 2010, pp. 97–126.

Ssunha. "[Urban Planning News] Seoul Opens a 'New 31,000 ㎡' Underground City' from City Hall to Sejong-Daero." 서울정책아카이브 *Seoul Solution*, Seoul Metropolitan Government, 22 Nov. 2016, www.seoul solution.kr/en/content/urban-planning-news-seoul-opens-%E2%80% 98new-31000%E3%8E%A1-underground-city%E2%80%99-city-hall-sejong-daero.

Statistics Korea. "Kosis Korean Statistical Information Service." *Statistical Database Population Census*, https://kosis.kr/eng/statisticsList/statistics ListIndex.do?menuId=M_01_01&vwcd=MT_ETITLE&parmTabId= M_01_01#content-group.

Statistics Korea. "Population & Households by Administrative District 1990." *Kosis*, Statistics Korea, 13 Mar. 2018, https://kosis.kr/statHtml/statHtml.do? orgId=101&tblId=DT_1IN9001&conn_path=I2&language=en.

Stoll, Katrina, and Scott Lloyd. *Infrastructure as Architecture: Designing Composite Networks*. Berlin: Jovis, 2010, p. 4.

"Superilles." *Bienvenido a Superilles | Superilles*, 2022, https://ajuntament. barcelona.cat/superilles/es/.

Susteren, Arjen van. *Metropolitan World Atlas*. Rotterdam: 010 Publishers, 2007.

"Terauchi ch'ongdog ŭi hunsi" [Instruction of Terauchi, the Government-General], *Maeil sinbo*, Apr. 14, 1914.

Transportation Metro Policy, et al. *Introduction of the Rapid Urban Railway System Construction of Subway Line 9*. Seoul: The Seoul Institute, 2017, pp. 1–8.

Trummer, Peter. *Peter Trummer*, www.petertrummer.com/.

Tschumi, Bernard. *Architecture and Disjunction*. Cambridge, MA: MIT Press, 2001.

"Underground Shopping Center: Global_main_en>Facility Management." *Underground Shopping Center | global_main_en>Facility Management*, Seoul Facilities Corporation, www.sisul.or.kr/global/main/en/sub/shopping center.jsp.

Ungers, Oswald M., et al. *Cities Within the City: Proposals by the Sommer Akademie for Berlin*. Ithaca, NY: Cornell University, 1978, pp. 82–97.

Ungers, O. M., et al. *The City in the City: Berlin: A Green Archipelago*. Zurich: Lars Müller Publishers, 2013.

United Nations, Department of Economic and Social Affairs Population Division. *World Urbanization Prospects the 2018 Revision*, United Nations, 2019, pp. 1–103.

"Urban Atlas 2018." *Copernicus*, 6 Oct. 2021, https://land.copernicus.eu/local/urban-atlas/urban-atlas-2018.

"Urbanization Planning of Seoul." 서울정책아카이브 *Seoul Solution*, 30 Aug. 2021, www.seoulsolution.kr/en/node/2375.

Urban Planning, and Sun-Wung Kim. *Urban Planning & Management*, The Seoul Institute, 2017, pp. 1–20.

Urban Planning, and Hyeon-Seok Min. *Sewun Mall Development Plan*, Seoul Metropolitan Government, 2017, pp. 1–11.

Varnelis, Kazys. "Programming After Program: Archizoom's No Stop City." *Praxis*, vol. 8, Dec. 2018, pp. 82–91.

Vergara, Victor. "Key Challenges to Urban Infrastructures." *Coursera*, École Polytechnique Fédérale De Lausanne, 2017, www.coursera.org/learn/managing-urban-infrastructures-1/lecture/26uqR?t=0.

Von Kempler, James. "Lotte World Tower: Seoul's First Supertall." *Council on Tall Buildings and Urban Habitat*, no. 1, 2018, pp. 12–19.

Waldheim, Charles. *Landscape as Urbanism: A General Theory*. New York: Princeton University Press, 2016.

Waldheim, Charles. *The Landscape Urbanism Reader*. New York: Princeton Architectural Press, 2006.

Weiss, Marion, and Michael A. Manfredi. *Public Natures: Evolutionary Infrastructures*. New York: Princeton Architectural Press, 2015.

Wigley, Mark. *Constant's New Babylon: The Hyper-Architecture of Desire*. Rotterdam: 010 Publishers, 1998, p. 93.

"World Urbanization Prospects 2018 – More Megacities in the Future | Multimedia Library – United Nations Department of Economic and Social Affairs." *United Nations*, United Nations, 16 May 2018, www.un.org/development/desa/publications/graphic/world-urbanization-prospects-2018-more-megacities-in-the-future.

Woo-hyun, Shim. "GS E&C's XI Named Top Apartment Brand in Korea for 2nd Year." *The Korea Herald*, The Korea Herald, 8 Nov. 2017, www.koreaherald.com/view.php?ud=20171108000695.

Wright, Frank Lloyd. *Broadacre City*. Tucson, AZ: University of Arizona Press, 1995.

Wright, Frank Lloyd. "Broadacre City. A New Community Plan." *Architectural Record*, vol. 77, Apr. 1935, pp. 243–254.

Yang, Jae-Sub. "Seoul's Urban Redevelopment Policy." *서울정책아카이브 Seoul Solution*, 10 Feb. 2017, https://seoulsolution.kr/en/content/seoul%E2%80%99s-urban-redevelopment-policy.

Yim, Haksoon. "Cultural Identity and Cultural Policy in South Korea." *The International Journal of Cultural Policy*, vol. 8, no. 1, 2002, pp. 37–48.

Yun, Jieheerah. *Globalizing Seoul: The City's Cultural and Urban Change*. Abingdon, Oxfordshire: Routledge, Taylor & Francis Group, 2018.

Züger, Mirjam, and Kees Christiaanse. *The Potato PLAN Collection: 40 Cities through the Lens of Patrick Abercrombie*. Rotterdam: nai010 Publishers, 2018.

Index